Making Money in China:

China Business Guide and Contacts

The Internationalist

www.internationalist.com

Titles Featured in the Business Guides Series

MAKING MONEY IN CHINA: Key Business
Contacts and Addresses

MAKING MONEY IN CHINA: China Business
Guide and Contacts

MAKING MONEY IN CHINA: China Country
Guide for Businesses

MAKING MONEY IN RUSSIA: Russia Country
Guide for Businesses

MAKING MONEY IN EXPORTING: A
Complete Guide to the Business of Exporting

The Internationalist® _____

International Business, Investment, and Travel

Published by:
The Internationalist Publishing Company
96 Walter Street/Suite 200
Boston MA 02131, USA
Tel: 617-354-7722
www.internationalist.com
PN@internationalist.com

Welcome to the **Making Money in China** series:

The key to a successful business is knowing the markets. MAKING MONEY IN CHINA: CHINA BUSINESS GUIDE AND CONTACTS offers executives, investors, and entrepreneurs the need-to-know information about doing business in China.

Written as an in-depth, straightforward reference guide, this book lists key information about the Chinese market, its challenges, and opportunities. It then looks into a dozen of China's leading industries, their backgrounds, current situation, and projected course.

MAKING MONEY IN CHINA: CHINA BUSINESS GUIDE AND CONTACTS concludes with a comprehensive list of companies and their primary information. Supplied are company logos, contacts, addresses, and brief summaries of any specialties.

Whether you are looking to break into international business or need to update your knowledge on Chinese markets— this comprehensive guide is for you.

The Internationalist

Contents

Intellectual Property Rights (IPR)

Due Diligence

Scams

Accounting, Auditing and Tax Services

Advertising

Banking and Financial services

Business Administration Services

Business Consulting

Business Development

Customs Brokerage

Distributors, Sales Agents and Importers

Education and Training Services

Environmental Services

Export Management

Hospitals, Clinics and Health Services

Legal Services

Manufacturing and Industrial Production Services

Market Research

Marketing, Public Relations and Sales

Office Rental

Other Business Services

Patent and Trademark Law Services

Product Standards, Testing, and Certification

Market Overview

China responded quickly to the global economic downturn in 2008 and, as a result of a combination of monetary, fiscal, and bank-lending measures China's GDP grew 9.2 percent in 2009 and an impressive 10.3 percent in 2010. Projections are for the GDP growth to slow slightly in 2011 to between 9 and 9.5 percent.

Accompanying the rise in China's GDP, U.S. exports to China increased in 2010 by over 32 percent to almost $92 billion. Of course, China's exports to the U.S. also increased by 23 percent, leading to a balance of trade deficit of $273 billion. After falling in 2009, the trade imbalance with China is now on the rise again. China remains the U.S.'s second largest trading partner after Canada.

After near zero percent inflation in 2009, in 2010 consumer price index rose 3.3 percent, exceeding the authorities' target of 3.0 percent. Inflation reached 5.1 percent in December 2010, alarming authorities who undertook a multipronged effort to bring real estate prices, food prices and monetary liquidity driven by bank lending under greater control.

Inbound FDI rebounded after a dip in 2009, rising 17.4 percent in 2010 to almost $106 billion. China is the world's second largest recipient of FDI after the United States.

China stands as the world's third largest market for luxury goods behind Japan and the United States, and some studies estimate that there are now more than 200 million Chinese citizens with a per capita income over USD 8,000. Over the next several years, most economists predict a surge in the number of people achieving true middle class status.

Despite these remarkable changes, China is still a developing country with significant economic divisions between urban and rural areas, albeit one with vast potential. The numbers of migrant workers continues to remain high, with the number of laborers employed outside their hometowns at approximately 150 million in 2009. This number has appeared to remain static, however, with some areas, especially in the East, reporting shortages of such laborers and tightening wage situations. As of 2010, the per-capita disposable income of urban residents was RMB 19,109 yuan (USD 2,895), and the per-capita disposable income of rural residents stood at RMB 5,919 (USD 897).

Market Challenges

In addition to the large multinationals which continue to earn impressive returns on their exports to and investments in China's market, American SMEs are also active here. FCS counsels American companies that to be a success in China, they must thoroughly investigate the market, take heed of product standards, pre-qualify potential business partners and craft contracts that assure payment and minimize misunderstandings between the parties. Stumbling blocks foreign companies often run into while doing business in China can be grouped into these broad categories:

- China often lacks predictability in its business environment. China's current legal and regulatory system can be opaque, inconsistent, and often arbitrary. Implementation of the law is inconsistent. Lack of effective Chinese government protection of intellectual property rights is a particularly damaging issue for many American companies. Both those that operate in China and those that do not have had their product IP stolen by Chinese companies.
- China has a government that, in some sectors of the economy, could be called mercantilist. China has made significant progress toward a market-oriented economy, but parts of its bureaucracy still seek to protect local firms, especially state-owned firms, from imports, while encouraging exports.
- China retains much of the apparatus of a planned economy. A five-year program sets economic goals, strategies, and targets. The State and the Communist Party directly manage the only legal labor union. The understanding of free enterprise and competition is incomplete in some sectors and political connections

or goals at times trump commercially-based decisions.

- Certain industrial sectors in China are prone to over-investment, leading to over-capacity, over-production, and declining prices in affected industries.

Continued economic reform is essential for China to achieve high levels of economic growth. China's own leaders recognize a more balanced economy relying more on domestic demand and development of the service sector are essential for China to become a mature economic power. However, companies must deal with the current environment in a realistic manner. Risk must be clearly evaluated. If a company determines that the risk is too great, it should seek other markets.

Market Opportunities

The growth of imports from the United States in many key sectors, such as energy, chemicals, transportation, medical equipment, construction, machinery and a range of services, suggests that China will remain an important and viable market for a wide range of products and services. With growing numbers of Chinese traveling abroad for education and leisure purposes, China's contribution to U.S. educational institutions and the tourism industry is increasingly important as well.

Education and Training

Overview

U.S. colleges and universities remain the preferred overseas destination for Chinese students and in 2010, Chinese students surpassed Indian students to become the most populous foreign students in the United States. Short-term training programs, technical schools and workshops in specialized fields as well as business education are particularly sought after. U.S. educational organizations can also sell teaching materials and equipment, convey the latest methodologies and case studies, exchange faculty, and provide educational consulting services.

Sub-Sector Best Prospects

In academic year 20009/10, roughly 128,000 Chinese students travelled to the United States to study. That constitutes a 30 percent increase from the previous academic year and the largest increase in the number of Chinese students going to the United States this decade. This 30 percent increase follows a 21 percent increase the previous academic year.

Year	# of Students from China to the U.S.	% Change From Previous Year
2009/10	127. 628	29.9%
2008/09	98,235	21.1%
2007/08	81,127	19.8%
2006/07	67,723	8.2%
2005/06	62,582	0.1%

Source: Institute of International Education

There's no doubt that the desire by Chinese students to enroll in U.S. institutions is high, fueled by increasing disposable incomes. Although the majority of Chinese students are still pursuing degrees in business, engineering and sciences, there appears to be an increase in demand for vocational classes and utilization of community colleges to upgrade skills to increase earning potential as well.

U.S. institutions will have to remain active in the promotion of American education in China, as competition for Chinese students from other English-speaking countries increases and as the expansion of the domestic education market in China creates an increasing number of opportunities for students to pursue higher education without leaving China. With this in mind, University admissions officers should be aware of and counsel prospective students on visa procedures affecting travel to the United States.

A common approach used by U.S. schools to recruit Chinese students is through local education agents. Over one thousand education agents are estimated to exist in China, with about 400 of them having obtained proper licensing from the Ministry of Education. U.S. schools are encouraged to carefully vet education agents before engaging their services. Bear in mind that the industry lacks sufficient oversight and complaints about education agents are common. The Commercial Section of the U.S. Embassy and U.S. Consulates can assist U.S. schools to vet education agents.

The U.S. footprint in China for educational services is dominated by U.S. universities, but other forms of training do well, in particular, management and English language training. Most local firms actively outsource these training needs. As a result, one can easily find courses throughout the country on leadership, team building, and people management. English language schools are also prevalent and proving to be a lucrative business. However, entering this market is quite costly. A local presence is a must and the market has a preference for instructors with Chinese language capabilities.

Marine Industries

This section covers the use and development of the various sea-related industries, including shipbuilding, ports, pleasure boats, sea communications and transportation, offshore oil and gas, sea-related chemicals and sea fisheries, etc.

China has seen rapid development of its marine industry over the past few years. China has more than 3 million square kilometers of water territory, with more than 1,400 harbors and 210,000 cargo ships. As the world's largest exporter, China has become a center of maritime activity, and China's major state-owned shipping and shipbuilding companies are among the world's largest. According to the Ministry of Land and Resources of the P.R.C., the marine industry will gradually become one of the pillars of China's economy.

According to the statistics of China Customs, China's total ship import and export values reached US$30.8 billion in 2009, of which ship imports accounted for US$2.4 billion. Trade volume could reach a historic high of approximately US$ 40 billion in 2010. However, oceanic pollution and the industry's structural imbalances, currency appreciation and cost increases continue to present challenges for the development of the marine industry.

Sub-Sector Best Prospects

Best prospects in China's marine industries include shipbuilding and marine engineering, recreational marine, and port related accessories and sea transportation.

Shipbuilding

Chinese shipbuilding deliveries and ship orders in hand have enjoyed fast growth for seven consecutive years and the country is currently ranked second in the world in both categories. According to statistics from the China Shipbuilding Industry Association, China's shipbuilding output was 42.43 million deadweight tons (DWT) in 2009, rising 47% from 2008. According to statistics issued by Clarkson, a UK consultant, Chinese shipbuilding deliveries were 56.76 million deadweight tons from January to November of 2010, with an increase of 55.4% compared with the same period in 2009. New ship orders were 26 million deadweight tons in 2009, which was down 55% compared with the same period in 2008. The market share of Chinese shipbuilding output, new ship orders and ship orders in hand respectively accounted for 34.8%, 61.6% and 38.5% of the world's totals in 2009. (Sources: Analysis on China's Shipbuilding Industry by China Shipbuilding Industry Association)

Although the China shipbuilding industry has enjoyed remarkable growth, the global financial crisis clearly hit the shipbuilding industry hard, such that new orders continue to decline in number and the currency appreciation and cost increases will impact the profits of China's shipbuilding companies in the long term.

The country plans to build three major shipbuilding bases in the Bohai Gulf area, East China Sea and South China Sea. When completed in 2015, the Changxing base will be the largest shipyard in the world with annual shipbuilding capacity reaching eight million tons.

In February 2009, China's State Council approved the revitalization plan for the Chinese shipbuilding industry. According to the plan, the government will encourage financial institutions to expand financing to purchasers of ships and extend financial support for domestic buyers of long-range ships until 2012. The plan will also support the industry by stabilizing production, growing domestic market demand, developing marine engineering equipment, supporting consolidation of the industry through mergers and acquisitions and technical innovations.

China needs high-technology, machinery and management tools for the shipbuilding industry. The best prospects for shipbuilding include: raw materials; coating equipment and coating materials; computer aided design (CAD) software and associated technologies for ship design and construction; equipment maintenance; Global Positioning Systems (GPS), navigation and on-board computer systems; cutting and welding technology and related equipment. China has routinely sought foreign design support for large marine engineering projects, but to date has relied heavily on European and Asian firms. With marine engineering projects a targeted area of growth in the industry revitalization plan, and with U.S. expertise in offshore energy projects, there will be increasing opportunities for U.S. design firms in this segment.

Recreational Marine industry

With the rapid growth of the economy, China's recreational marine market is forecast to expand sharply in the coming years. In 2010, China imported over 80 million USD worth of yachts and pleasure vessels, which was an increase of 138% compared with 2009. (China Customs) Based on the confidence that pleasure boats will become one aspect of the country's expanding upper- and the middle-class life style, provincial governments, property developers and boat builders are all investing heavily in this industry. Business experts estimate that the market will pick up speed in the next few years, and the overall market size may reach US$10 billion over the next decade, which presents significant opportunities for the export of U.S. pleasure boats, accessories, marina planning and construction materials. (China Boat Industry and Trade Association)

Although there are presently only a handful of marinas in China, dozens more are under construction or in planning. Many luxury residences in major cities incorporate waterways and boating facilities in their developments. The Shanghai Government has decided to build marinas and cruising shipping centers along the downtown riverfront as part of the efforts to remake Shanghai into a world-class city. Other cities and areas that either have on-going marina projects, or are in the planning process, include Zhoushan, Qingdao ,Dalian, Ningbo, Beihai, Dongguan, Shengzhen and Hainan Island.

Port construction and Sea-Transportation

China is allocating significant capital for port and waterway construction to meet significant growth in freight volume. Since 2004, China has stepped up its construction of ports. China's port throughput is increasing at exponential rates, reflecting foreign trade growth. Eight ports in mainland China, namely Shanghai, Shenzhen, Qingdao, Tianjin, Guangzhou, Xiamen, Ningbo and Dalian, are included among the 30 top container harbors in the world. The port of Shanghai is by far the busiest one in the world. The cargo turnover of Shanghai port exceeded 650 million tons and container throughput reached 29 million TEU in 2010. Both of these two indexes have exceeded Singapore as the world's largest port.

To facilitate global trade, most ports in China are putting emphasis on expanding capacity and upgrading port facilities as well as in the modernization of operations. The products and technologies in high demand are Vessel Traffic Management Information Systems, laser-docking systems, terminal tractors, dredging equipment and security equipment for ports and vessels to enable them to comply with the International Ship and Port Security Code (ISPS).

China is building more deep-water berths to handle the larger fifth and sixth generation container vessels. The largest project is the construction of Yangshan deep-water port, approximately 20 miles offshore from Shanghai and linked to the mainland by a 32.5-kilometer causeway bridge. The master plan calls for the completion of 50 berths by 2020, which will cost over US$10billion. It also includes a logistics park and new harbor city on the mainland. Lianyungang, a northern port city in Jiangsu Province, is racing to build an international port after winning State Council approval to construct a 300,000DWT(Dead Weight Ton) deepwater channel and a 300,000 DWT berth for handling crude oil and ore, in conjunction with development of the neighboring Yangshan Deep Water Port in Shanghai and the existing Ningbo Port.

Opportunities

China's marine equipment industry currently lags behind the shipbuilding industry. Equipment that is in high demand includes machinery, key electric-mechanical equipment, communications systems, diesel engine crank-shafts and their key components, high-powered diesel engines, ship superstructures, products that facilitate the deep-sea operation of ocean exploration ships, high-grade steel plates and section bars, and environmentally friendly paint. Other potential prospects for shipbuilding can be seen in markets for coating equipment, CAD (computer-aided design) software and associated technology for ship design and construction, equipment maintenance, high-tech equipment (GPS, navigation, on-board computer systems, etc.), cutting and welding technology, and related equipment.

Pleasure boats are one of the best prospects for exporters. China's recreational marine industries are poised to expand rapidly in the coming years. Confident that pleasure boats will become incorporated into the lifestyle of China's growing wealthy classes, provincial governments, property developers and boat builders are all investing heavily in this rising industry, presenting significant opportunities for U.S. exporters of pleasure boats, accessories, marina planning services and construction materials.

Air Pollution

Overview

Air pollution is one of the biggest environmental challenges for public health in China today. The source of air pollution in Chinese cities has gradually changed from conventional coal combustion to a mixture of coal-combustion and motor-vehicle emissions.

According to the Ministry of Environmental Protection, China's air pollution increased in 2010 for the first time since 2005, due in major part to an increase in motor vehicles and a rise in construction and industrial projects. It reports that the number of "good air quality days" in 113 major cities across the nation, dropped 0.3 percentage points in the first six months of 2010 compared with the same time period in 2009.

According to the Ministry of Environmental Protection (MEP), one-third of 113 major cities failed air quality tests in 2009, in large part due to motor vehicle emissions. The MEP also revealed that in 2009 the number of cars owned by Chinese citizens jumped to 170 million, a 9.3 percent increase year on year, and 25 times the car ownership figures from 1980. The volume of pollutants generated by motor vehicles across China in 2009 amounted to 51.4 million tons, with cars contributing a majority percentage.

Among traditional pollutants in waste gas emission, SO2, soot and industrial dust are the three main categories. Though showing a better tendency than in previous years, the total SO2 discharge in China was still 22.14 million tons in 2009. Despite the decrease of industrial SO2 discharge (18.65 million tons), municipal SO2 discharge is still on the rise. The situation is the same with soot discharge. Municipal soot discharge rose by 5.3% in 2009 from the previous year. (See chart below)

	SO2 Discharge (10,000 tons)			Soot Discharge (10,000 tons)			Industrial Dust (10,000 tons)
Year	Total	Industrial	Municipal	Total	Industrial	Municipal	Discharge
2005	2,549.3	2,168.4	381	1,182.5	948.9	233.6	911.2
2006	2,588.8	2,234.8	354	1,088.8	864.5	224.3	808.4
2007	2,468.1	2,140	328.1	986.6	771.1	215.5	698.7
2008	2,321.2	1,991.3	329.9	901.6	670.7	230.9	584.9
2009	2,214.4	1,865.9	348.5	847.7	604.4	243.3	523.6

Source: data from "2010 China Statistical Yearbook" published on September, 2010.

The Chinese government's attention to the dangers that result from the generation of nitrogen oxides (NOx) has increased in recent years. On January 27, 2010, the Ministry of Environmental Protection issued their "Notice of Fossil-Fired Power Plant NOx Emission Prevention and Treatment Policy." This official government policy sets the framework for NOx reduction actions to be taken under the nation's 12th Five Year Plan, which began on January 1, 2011.

The policy set forth in this Notice applies to all coal-fired power plants and co-generation units that are 200 MW or larger, except in designated "Focus Areas" where it applies to all units regardless of size. In addition, all new, rebuilt or units that have undergone expansion should install Low-NOx Combustion Technologies as a first step. For units already in operation, if the NOx emission levels do not meet emission standards, then they must install flue gas de-NOx technology.

Quantity of NOx Emissions

	2004*	2005*	2010**	2020**
Annual Coal Consumption	1.5 billion tons	1.6 billion tons	to 2 billion tons	to 3 billion tons
GW Electricity Capacity	440.7 (350 Fossil)	508	670	1000 (580 Fossil)
Annual NOx Emissions (million tons)	14	16	25	28.7 to 30

Source: China Electricity Council

*Annual Coal Consumptions in 2004 and 2005 are approximate figures.

**2010 and 2020 numbers are based on estimation.

China has also begun measures to reduce emissions of carbon dioxide (CO_2). Although China is unlikely to agree to implement any absolute cuts on these emissions in the near future, the government's decision in late 2009 to try to cut its 'carbon intensity' (the amount of carbon emitted per unit of GDP) by 40-45% from the 2005 level by 2020 represents a big step forward and should lead to a greater emphasis on clean energy over the next decade. Even with the new tough targets, overall CO_2 emissions could still end up rising sharply over the next few decades.

In his speech at the 2009 Conference on China Environmental Monitoring Work, Vice Minister Wu Xiaoqing outlined the top priorities of environmental monitoring work for the 12th Five-year Plan (2011-2015). Air monitoring equipment suppliers should focus on the below market opportunities in China from 2011-2015:

- Expand existing monitoring networks to rural areas
- Build up monitoring capacity to achieve total volume monitoring of pollutants
- Establish an environmental monitoring information publishing and releasing platform.

(On January 1, 2011, the Central government began releasing hourly readings on levels of sulfur dioxide, nitrogen dioxide, and coarse particulate matter to the public on the 113 cities in China's national air quality data network)

The various plans mentioned above will trigger commercial opportunities in the coming 2-5 years as the government tries its best to build up environmental monitoring capacity and upgrade China's monitoring technology as a critical way to support the overall environmental cleanup. Strict measures such as nation-wide inspections and professional training will undoubtedly lead to a surge in the need for air monitoring equipment upgrades, technology introduction and technical training, thus generating tremendous market opportunities in the years to come.

U.S. firms are facing both domestic and third-country competition, including, government-subsidized Japanese and European competitors. Though growing very fast, the domestic industry is still in an early stage of development due to its short development history, loose management, inadequate financing and poor enforcement. U.S. air monitoring equipment is well received and often considered high-quality in terms of data accuracy, timeliness and system endurance. To grasp the opportunities, U.S. companies should develop suitable market entry and pricing strategies to beat the fierce competition in the market.

Commodity	Description	Unit: United States Dollars (millions)			% Share			% Change
		2007	2008	2009	2007	2008	2009	2009/2008
Air Monitoring Products		378.03	503.14	467.50	100	100	100	-7.08
90261000	Instruments / Apparatus For Measure / Checking Liquid	86.87	123.67	113.46	22.98	24.58	24.27	-8.26

90272011	Gas Chromatography Instruments	61.91	82.50	82.27	16.38	16.4	17.6	-0.27
90269000	Parts And Accessories Of Instruments / Appliances	76.27	92.63	77.69	20.18	18.41	16.62	-16.13
90268000	Instruments / Apparatus F Measure / Check Liquid / Gas	38.65	39.33	46.30	10.22	7.82	9.9	17.73
90271000	Gas Or Smoke Analysis Apparatus	38.19	50.69	45.62	10.1	10.07	9.76	-10
90272019	Other Chromatography Instruments	18.27	35.95	37.18	4.83	7.14	7.95	3.43
90262090	Other Instruments / Apparatus For Measuring	31.08	42.98	33.52	8.22	8.54	7.17	-22.02
90262010	Pressure / Differential Pressure Transducers	18.28	22.02	16.83	4.84	4.38	3.6	-23.6
90272020	Electrophoresis Instruments	7.75	12.73	13.22	2.05	2.53	2.83	3.86
90281090	Other Gas Meters	.66	.59	13.45	0.17	0.12	0.29	125.16
90281010	Coal Gas Meters	.79	.38	.67	0.02	0.01	0.01	74.79

China's Imports and Exports of Air Monitoring Equipment

Unit: USD millions

	2007	2008	2009	2010 estimated	2011 estimated	2012 estimated
Total Market Size	N/A	N/A	N/A	N/A	N/A	N/A
Total Local Production	N/A	N/A	N/A	N/A	N/A	N/A
Total Exports	703.79	942.36	824.83	970.38	1,141.62	1,34.3.08
Total Imports	1,247.11	1,606.48	1,493.35	1,799.21	2,167.72	2,611.71
Imports from the U.S.	378.03	503.14	467.50	584.38	730.47	913.08
Exchange Rate: 1 USD	7.31	6.84	6.83	6.77	6.55	6.55

Source: Chinese Customs

Sub-Sector Best Prospects

The demand for modern environmental monitoring instruments in China remains high. In particular, there is an urgent need for advanced NOx emission reduction equipment, automatic monitoring systems and on-line continuous monitoring systems.

Viable De-NOx Technologies

- Combustion Modification
- SNCR (Selective Non-Catalytic Reduction)
- CR ((Selective Catalytic Reduction))

- Combination Methods

Rising concerns about China's environment have led to a surge in demand for the following environmental monitoring instruments:

1. Automatic air monitoring systems on the ground: high value-added equipment which is automatic, multi-functional, instant, systematic, and intelligent is considered the most promising in China. Typical products are:

- On-line and/or automatic continuous emission monitoring systems for key pollution sources

- Carbon Monoxide (CO)
- Sulfur Dioxide (SO2)
- Nitrogen Oxides (NO-NO2-NOX)
- Ozone (O3)
- Particulate Matter (PM10/2.5)

- Automatic and continuous monitoring systems for organic pollutants

- Volatile Organic Compounds (VOCs)

- On-line dust monitors

- On-site portable emergency gas monitoring equipment

- Portable and personal particulate monitors

2. Remote monitoring systems: Investments will also increase for satellite ground systems and satellite image analysis systems to analyze the quality of the environment and changing long-term trends. China's emphasis on the protection of the ecological environment has created a great demand base for remote sensing satellites and monitoring equipment. The industry is gradually

transferring from ground monitoring only to both ground and remote monitoring. Potential segments include:

- Vehicle-borne equipment, such as mobile monitoring vans
- Ship-borne equipment
- Satellite-borne equipment and instruments, such as lesser radar monitors for pollution
- GSM/GPRS modem technology (allowing remote control and data retrieval from air quality monitoring stations located almost anywhere)

3. Quality Assurance (QA) and Quality Control (QC) laboratory equipment, which is needed in all monitoring stations and laboratories. Instruments include:

- SO2 analyzers
- NOX analyzers
- PM10 samplers
- PM2.5 samplers
- Dynamic gas dilution/mixing/calibration systems
- High precision flow meters

Opportunities

Since 1990, China has improved its environmental monitoring technology by introducing advanced foreign technology. U.S. air pollution control product exports to China have been rising steadily at about 10-15% with a sharp increase in 2008, registering a 24.8% rise over the previous year. While the amount of products imported in 2009 was down 7.08% from 2008, longer term trends still indicate potential for growth in the industry. This trend is expected to continue in the next couple of years as China maintains its effort to improve the air quality.

Though facing strong competition from Japan and European companies, U.S. environmental monitoring equipment, especially air monitoring equipment, has a good reputation for high quality, low maintenance, and endurance. Thus, there are many opportunities for American companies here in China. However, many important factors must be considered in order to remain competitive in the air monitoring market.

While value for money is ultimately the determining factor in Chinese purchasing decisions, access to appropriate officials, decision-makers and project information is also critical for success. In light of the potential market, U.S. firms would clearly benefit from having an environmental staff in China dedicated solely to maintaining and promoting environmental programs and leads. Furthermore, products need to be reasonably priced and developed specifically for Chinese market requirements.

<u>Major prospective buyers in China:</u>

Ministry of Environmental Protection (MEP):

MEP mandates rules, regulations, and emission standards for polluting enterprises and is responsible for establishing environmental monitoring networks all over the country and managing national environmental monitoring. MEP helps cities and counties establish monitoring stations, and works jointly with industrial ministries to establish environmental monitoring networks.

In 2008, when the former State Environment Protection Administration was upgraded to the Ministry of Environmental Protection, a new department – the Environment Monitoring Department was established, a clear signal that environmental monitoring is now a high government priority.

China National Environmental Monitoring Center:

The China National Environmental Monitoring Center (CNEMC) is directly affiliated with the MEP and is in charge of analysis and research of national environmental quality, management techniques, and monitoring data. It also provides scientific and technical support for the MEP.

Under the policy supervision of the MEP, environmental protection bureaus at the provincial administration levels are responsible for monitoring and enforcing compliance in this sector at the local level. Local EMCs at the provincial and municipal levels are in charge of monitoring, data collecting and analysis at the regional level.

National key pollution sources – 3715 enterprises (air):

In April 2009, MEP updated the list of National Key Pollutions Sources that are strictly under monitoring and control. Among the 6969 key pollution sources, 3715 are air polluting enterprises. These enterprises are required to equip themselves with on-line/real-time monitoring equipment such as continued emission control systems (CEMS). Installation of ambient air monitoring equipment is also required for surrounding areas of their manufacturing sites.

Major parameters measured include dust, soot, smoke, SO2, NOx, CO and flue gases. Among the 3715, power plants account for a major share, followed by some other heavily polluting enterprises listed below:

- Power plants
- Petrochemicals
- Refineries
- Building materials (cement especially) and
- Metallurgy

Green Building

China has the world's largest construction market. According to the Ministry of Housing and Urban-Rural Development (MOHURD), over the next decade, China will build half of the world's new buildings and is currently adding 2 billion square meters of floor space annually.

2011 was the first year of China's 12th Five-Year (2011-2015) plan for Economic and Social Development. In this plan, China is set to make the reduction of energy consumption and carbon dioxide emissions a "binding goal." Many provinces and cities have drafted their own enforcement plan, and many cities are planning to become an "eco-city" by not only retrofitting old buildings but also by building new low-carbon buildings. The U.S. Department of Energy and MOHURD are cooperating on green building research and pilot projects through the U.S. China Clean Energy Research Center.

Sub-Sector Best Prospects

Green building products that meet the new energy efficiency standards in new, unique or economically competitive ways have a potential market in China. Some of the best prospects for China's market are:

- Green-design techniques
- HVAC systems
- Solar products

- Grey water, water reuse systems, and landscape materials
- New building materials
- New technologies & products

According to the China Greentech Initiative 2010 report, the following building materials are targeted to become energy efficient products in China.

- Concrete: slag cement and fly-ash content; autoclaved aerated concrete
- Insulation: Expanded (EPS) and Extruded Polystyrene (XPS)
- Roofing: Reflective Systems, Vegetated Roofs, TPO membranes
- Windows and Doors: double-glazed, low-solar-gain, Low-E Glass
- Lighting: T-series light fixtures, CFL and LED bulbs
- HVAC: absorption chillers, variable frequency drives (VFD), energy recovery wheels, air purifying equipment
- In-door building materials: low-emission, thermal and noise reduction, and insulation
- Integrated designs

On December 2010, the Ministry of Finance, Ministry of Science and Technology, MOHURD, and the State Energy Bureau jointly announced government subsidies for solar roofing systems to promote the development of solar products in China. China's13 economic development zones were designated as demonstration areas.

Due to China's geographical structure, heat preservation, insulation, translucence, and ventilation are very important in China's different regions. For example, in northern China, it is imperative to reduce the energy consumed by heat production. Improvements in heat conservation in new and old buildings are vital to achieving this goal. New types of energy conservation products, such as wall-structure preservation products, and heat supply measuring systems have been used extensively in these areas.

Opportunities

The year 2011 marked the beginning of China's 12th Five-Year (2011-2015) Plan for Economic and Social Development. Many provinces and cities have drafted their own development plans.

For example:

According to Zhu Zhongyi, Vice Chairman of the China Real Estate Association, in every year of the plan, China plans to build 6 million units of commercial buildings, and 5 million units of affordable housing.

China will build over 40,000 kilometers of express rail lines, and over 85,000 kilometers of highway during China's 12th Five-Year period.

According to the "National Airport Allocation Plan", China will upgrade, expand and build 244 airports by the end of 2020. For example: Beijing's second capital airport will be located in Daxing County, Beijing. The airport is expected to be operational in 2015, and will serve 600 million passengers per year.

According to China Construction News, in 2011 MOHURD planned to build 10 million units of affordable housing (this figure is double the size of the China Real Estate Association's prediction). The total investment will be over $21 million (RMB 140million).

Xi'an City will build 3.73 million square meters of affordable housing, and Chongqing city will build 30 million square meters by the year 2013.

According to MOHURD's Qinghai branch, Qinghai province plans to invest $11.2 billion (RMB 74 billion) in real estate development by 2015.

By 2015, Nanchang city plans to build 231 key projects, the total investment of which will reach $23 billion (RMB 150 billion). Projects will include fast transportation systems with modern transportation hubs, bio-landscape gardens, and a renewable energy demonstration city.

By 2015, Hubei province plans to build 1,000 eco-demonstration towns and villages. The water supply pipe line will reach 98% of the province, the garbage treatment rate will reach 85%, and the urbanization rate will reach 52% in Hubei province.

Nanjing city plans to use geo-thermal technology in their buildings, and 60% of new buildings plan to include this technology by 2013.

During the 12th Five-Year period, Wuhan city plans to invest $2 billion (RMB13.1 billion) in green landscape projects.

Renewable Energy — Solar and Wind

Overview

Although China still relies on coal to produce more than two-thirds of its energy, it continues to rapidly increase renewable energy sources. China is now the world's largest producer of hydropower and in 2010 overtook the United States as the world leader in installed wind capacity. China is also the world's leading manufacturer of solar photovoltaic (PV) cells, but its domestic market remains immature. Renewable sources produce approximately 10% of China's energy, and the Chinese government expects to boost that share to at least 15% by 2020.

Sub-Sector Best Prospects

Solar:
China has large solar resources and is the world's leading manufacturer of solar PV and solar water heaters. China-manufactured PV accounted for nearly 50% of global supply in 2010, and China now produces over 70% of the world's solar water heaters. However, 95% of its solar panels are exported to countries with more favorable incentives. China has established a solar energy target of 20 GW of installed PV capacity by 2020 and 300 million m2 for solar water heating.

The government has used the concession process for utility-scale PV projects to help it set a price it deems appropriate for solar energy. In 2009, China issued its first tender for two 10 MW utility-scale solar power plants in Dunhuang, Gansu province. In 2010, the Chinese government initiated a second round of concession bids for 13 large-scale PV projects for a total of 280 MW. The projects are located in six western provinces: Shaanxi, Qinghai, Gansu, Inner Mongolia, Ningxia and Xinjiang.

Wind:

China has the largest wind resources in the world, with three-quarters offshore. According to the China Wind Energy Association, China's wind power capacity grew by more than

100% for 4 consecutive years from 2006. In 2010, wind power installation capacity reached 30 GW, and China overtook the United States to become the world's largest wind power market. China aims to have 150 GW of wind power capacity by 2020.

China has over 80 wind turbine manufacturers and 70 blade manufacturers. In 2009, three Chinese firms ranked among the top ten globally: Sinovel (No. 3), Goldwind (No.5) and Dongfang (No. 7). From 2008 to 2009, Chinese firms began to export turbines and components abroad. China's Central government recently issued offshore wind regulations, with a target of 30 GW installed capacity planned for 2020; however, many uncertainties remain about the viability of offshore wind in China.

Opportunities

Although China is already the world's largest supplier of photovoltaic cells, it exports approximately 90% of production with the domestic market still undeveloped. Utility-scale solar is being explored in remote western regions with plentiful land and solar resources. China's low-carbon development zones and eco-cities present significant opportunities. Crystalline silicon is favored in China due to the local manufacturing base, but there is growing interest in thin-film technology. Concentrated Solar Power (CSP) is new in China, but a niche market may open up in western regions. Chinese inverters and control boxes are less advanced and of lower quality than foreign-made components, presenting opportunities for U.S. companies.

Cutting-edge and high-quality technologies that drive down operating costs, improve wind farm efficiency, or support and enhance connectivity to the grid will play an important role in the growth of the wind industry. Opportunities also exist for companies that can help China more accurately assess wind resources. Materials technology, reliable high-performance controllers, and bearings are in critical need by Chinese manufacturers. Specialized coating products, particularly for offshore projects, could also present opportunities.

According to the China Greentech Initiative, primarily due to Chinese government policy objectives, the offshore wind sector should experience strong growth in the coming years.

Companies with offshore experience will find most opportunities in areas where there is limited or no domestic competition. This would include such things as bearings, composites, installation expertise, undersea cables, offshore electronics, foundations, generators, controls systems, and converters. Sinovel, for example, sources 20% of its 3- MW offshore turbine components from foreign vendors.

Safety and Security

Overview

Unit: USD millions

	2009	2010	2011 (estimated)	2012 (estimated)
Total Market Size	2,724	3,533	4,230	4,230
Total Local Production	2,367	3,088	3,790	3,790
Total Exports	217	202	210	210
Total Imports	575	648	650	650
Imports from the U.S.	153	143	140	150
Exchange Rate: 1 USD	6.83	6.77	6.55	6.55

Data Sources: China Customs, Zeefer Consulting

Over the last four years the annual compound growth rate of the safety/security equipment market in China was about 30 percent. In 2010, due to active demand in such fields as urban construction, road/transportation infrastructure development, finance, education and the military, the market for safety/security equipment reached USD 3.53 billion. This was up by 36 percent over the previous year, leading to a year-upon-year growth rate of 22.percent. The rapid development of the domestic safety and security equipment industry shows that this industry has an enormous market potential. Considering various domestic and international market factors, including the development of more and more product applications, assuming an average annual market growth rate of 20%, we predict the market will grow to $4.23 billion in 2011.

Sub-Sector Best Prospects

Much of the demand for safety and security equipment focuses on high-tech equipment, such as digital technology, security guard communications systems, network technology for inspection control systems, and emergency warning systems.

- Inspection Control Systems: This has been a high-growth area in recent years and remains very competitive. Panasonic, Samsung, Sony, JVC, and Sanyo dominate China's high-grade inspection control market.
- Security Guard Communication systems: China's domestic enterprises occupy the majority share in this sector, and foreign enterprises such as US companies BII and HID, the UK's TDSI, and Israel's DDS dominate the security guard communications import market.
- Emergency Warning Systems: There is great demand for intelligent airport systems. Foreign companies dominate the market for high-end products, leading the trend towards integrated safety and security systems.
- Detection Equipment: Since China's domestic manufacturers lack capacity to produce enough

equipment, foreign products in this field are in high demand.

Opportunities

The safety and security sector remains a highly regulated industry in China. In most cases, when local safety and security engineering companies are awarded tenders for large projects, they need to then source the required products. US exporters should look for opportunities to provide products by partnering with these local Chinese engineering firms which often have strong connections with the Chinese government. Moreover, such a partnership provides additional advantages in that these Chinese firms are often better positioned to more readily process and obtain all required certifications.

Aviation Market

Overview

Aircraft, Spacecraft, and related parts (HS Code 88) Unit: USD millions

	2008	2009	2010
Total Exports	1,640	941	1,265
Total Imports	10,152	10,693	12,399
Imports from the U.S.	3,956	5,378	5,899
Exchange Rate: 1 USD	6.84	6.83	6.77

Data Sources: Global Trade Atlas, Boeing Market Outlook, AVIC China Market Outlook

China is one of the world's fastest growing civil aviation markets. The industry has grown at double-digit rates for several years, and in 2009 passenger traffic grew nearly 20% to reach 230 million person-trips. Industry forecasts expect growth to remain strong over the medium term, averaging 7% over the next 20 years.

In order to keep pace with demand, China is forecast to require 4,330 new aircraft valued at $480 billion over the next 20 years. Most of these will be single-aisle aircraft designed for short-haul domestic travel. Commercial opportunities in the civil aviation market include final assembly and tier-one suppliers, small niche parts manufacturers, airport design and construction companies, and general aviation among others.

The Chinese face three key challenges that threaten to limit this growth: inadequate infrastructure, overly restrictive airspace, and lack of skilled human resources. In response to over-congestion at its largest airports, China announced plans to invest $64 billion for construction of 97 new airports by 2021. Then in November 2010, Chinese military and civilian authorities issued a joint statement outlining liberalization of airspace less than

4000 meters (13,000 feet) by 2020. Personnel training and capacity building are a priority for regulators, airlines, airport operators and manufacturers. US firms often use training programs to establish productive partnerships with Chinese clients. Associations such as the U.S.-China Aviation Cooperation Program (ACP) can serve as valuable vehicles for smaller firms to leverage similar opportunities.

Sub-Sector Best Prospects

Aircraft Parts: Manufacture and Repair
Aircraft parts (HS Code 8803) Unit: USD millions

	2008	2009	2010
Total Exports	1,193	850	966
Total Imports	1,228	1,155	1,446
Imports from the U.S.	697	488	545
Exchange Rate: 1 USD	6.84	6.83	6.77

Data Sources: Global Trade Atlas

China's import market for aircraft parts and components exceeded $1.4 billion in 2010, an increase of over 25% compared with last year. China's demand for aircraft parts can be attributed to a number of factors including an increasing capacity utilization rate, the age and expansion of China's aircraft fleet, and the domestic production and assembly of aircraft.

The average age of a commercial aircraft in China is four years, and as the fleet continues to age, it will require parts and equipment for routine maintenance and repair. Though there are a number of major domestic aircraft and parts manufacturers scattered throughout China, the sector is still underdeveloped, creating a strong demand for reliable imported products and technologies to ensure quality standards.

China's domestic aircraft part and assembly manufacturing sector is also growing. In addition to approximately 200 small aircraft parts manufacturers, there are also a number of regionally-based major manufacturers concentrated in Shanghai, Chengdu, Xi'an, Tianjin, Jiangxi and Shenyang. China's domestic manufacturing base is developing, as reflected by the commitments of large aircraft and engine manufactures to expand procurement in China over a long term. However, most highly technical and sophisticated parts and assemblies will continue to be imported until technical capabilities and production quality meet international standards. At the present time, domestic manufacturers do not have the ability to produce all of the qualified materials and parts.

Airports

China currently has 166 civil aviation airports, including the world's second busiest in Beijing, with plans to expand aggressively to 244 by 2020. The government announced plans to invest $64 billion to build and improve 97 airports by 2021, including 78 green field projects. The expansion will place 80% of China's population and 96% of its GDP within 100 kilometers of the nearest airport, greatly enhancing the potential for aviation growth.

The airport system at present is highly concentrated, with top airports suffering from major congestion. The top three airports, Beijing, Shanghai and Guangzhou, account for a third of all traffic, while the top 14 airports handle two-thirds of total traffic nationwide. Local industry estimates indicate that 40 of China's airports are already at or near capacity, with another 29 expected to reach this limit within the next two years. To relieve congestion, China opened 14 new airports in the two-year period from 2009-2010.

Construction of the long-awaited second airport in Beijing could likely begin in 2011. The airport is expected to be built in the southern part of China's capital, primarily servicing domestic flights while Beijing's Capital International Airport will continue its role as China's leading international hub. The Planning Department of CAAC disclosed that the review and selection of the site is already underway and a research group was formed by the CAAC to oversee the initial plan of the proposed airport construction project.

International companies will have opportunities to participate in both the airport design and in the infrastructure construction. Qualified companies may be approved to compete with domestic companies via a bidding process for design, consultation, surveillance, management, and construction of designated civil airport projects. So far, the Beijing Capital Airport, Shanghai Pudong Airport, Shanghai Hongqiao Airport, Shenzhen Huangtian Airport, and Guangzhou's new Baiyun Airport were all designed by foreign companies.

Ground service is another area in which foreign companies can actively participate. Beijing Capital Airport, Guangzhou Baiyun Airport, and Chengdu Shuangliu Airport have all established joint ventures with foreign partners (Singapore, Indonesia and UK) in ground services. Shanghai Airport Ground cooperated with Cargo Warehouse and Lufthansa set up a joint venture. China Air Oil Supply Corporation (CAOSC) has established many joint ventures with foreign companies to provide aviation oil supply services.

General Aviation

General Aviation (GA) remains an underdeveloped part of China's aviation industry. Local industry contacts estimate that China has only about 1,000 GA aircraft, compared with more than 220,000 in the US. Of this total, only about 100 are large business jets, equivalent to the total for the State of Maryland.

Strict military control over roughly 70% of all Chinese airspace is the largest single factor limiting growth of this industry. A welcome change came in November 2010 when civilian and military authorities issued a joint reform document calling for liberalization of low altitude airspace under 4,000 meters (13,000 feet).

Implementation of the reform will roll out in three stages, starting with an Experimental Phase in Guangzhou and Shenyang. The policy outlines a national rollout by 2015, and a final deepening and consolidation by 2020. While the details remain vague, this policy shift indicates clear support for GA and should have large and positive impacts on the sector. Market potential is vast. In the southern province of Guangdong alone (one of the two pilot areas), market demand is estimated at 200-250 aircraft worth $1 – 1.25 billion.

Automotive Components Market

Overview

China has become the largest automotive market in the world in terms of the volume of manufacturing and sales in 2010, with 18.3 million vehicles manufactured and 18.06 million sold in the country, representing a 32.4% annual increase from 2009. China imported $58.2 billion worth of automotive components in 2010. Growth in the motorcycle market is still limited by a general prohibition on motorcycles in China's large cities.

China has about 6,000 automotive-related enterprises in five sectors: motor vehicle manufacturing, vehicle refitting, motorcycle production, auto engine production, and auto parts manufacturing. This includes approximately 100 OEMs, with 40 producing passenger vehicles, and over 4000 registered auto parts/accessories companies. All tiers of the industry are being driven by the booming sales of the OEM sector. Nearly 80% of the revenue for the auto parts and accessories market is through new vehicle sales. However, revenue from the after-market is increasing rapidly.

Shanghai and its surrounding provinces (Zhejiang, Jiangsu, and Anhui) are the centers for component manufacturing, representing around 44% of national production. Shanghai is home to Shanghai General Motors, Delphi, Visteon, and other notable American automotive companies and, as such, provides a good starting point for U.S. automotive component exporters to begin to explore the Chinese market. Other major automotive centers in China include Guangzhou (South China), Chongqing (West China), Changchun (Northeast China), Wuhan (Central China), and Tianjin (North China).

Key indicators for six emerging markets

Region	Population (Million)	GDP (2009, $B)	GDP per capita ($, 2009)	Import value (2009, $M)	% share of total imports	Import CAGR*, 2006–09	Total Motor Vehicle Production (2009, $B)

Changchun	7.6	42.5	5,526	2,622	16%	16%	1,220
Tianjin	12	112	9,136	1,595	9.7%	6%	600
Wuhan	9.1	67	7,362	1,077	6%	0.2%	490
Nanjing	6.3	63	8,252	715	4.3%	17%	400
Chongqing	28.6	97.5	3,420	684	4%	2%	1,190
Shenzhen	9	120	13,581	78	0.5%	3%	450
China	1,335	4,932	3,694	16,516	100%	11%	13,790

Source: TDC trade, US Commercial Service, World Trade Atlas (China Customs) and China Automotive Industry Yearbook.
*CAGR = compound annual growth rate

With 47% of all automotive component imports in 2009, Japan remains the largest exporter of automotive components to China. Germany and South Korea are the second and third exporter of automotive components, accounting for 22% and 11% respectively. The U.S. is the fourth-largest exporter with only 4% of the market. Some of the obstacles that U.S companies encounter are: 1) Good price but lack of the most advanced technology. 2) Difficult to compete with Japanese and Korean suppliers since Japanese and Korean OEMs normal only import from their home-country suppliers.

China total import of parts and accessories (HS8708), $M

HS Code	Description	2006	2007	2008	2009	2010	CAGR '06-'09

870829	M VHCL BODY PTS/ACC	2,459	1,946	2,201	2,322	3,214	
87083011	BRAKE, SERVO-BRAKE	780	845	781	805	1,116	1%
870840	GEAR BOXES	2,017	3,274	3,979	4,986	7,304	35.2%
870899	OTHER 8708	2,662	2,582	1,833	1,753	2,120	
Total		7,918	8,647	8,794	9,866	13,754	7.6%

Source: JLJ analysis on data from World Trade Atlas

Sub-Sector Best Prospects

Engines, especially engines smaller than 1.6 liters, for motor vehicles and motorcycles (made by U.S. companies in China);

New energy-related, such as technology and products related to hybrids and electrical cars, especially for buses;

Three-way catalytic devices;

ABS;
Automatic gear boxes;

Braking systems;

Machinery, tools, testing equipment for OEM products;

Auto and motorcycle casting blanks;

Key, high-tech automotive parts and components including disc-type braking assemblies, drive axle assemblies, automatic transmission boxes, engine admission superchargers, engine displacement control devices, electric servo steering systems, viscous continuous shaft devices (for four-wheel drive), air shock absorbers, air suspension frames, hydraulic tappets, and compound meters.

Auto electronic devices and instruments (including control systems for engines, chassis and vehicle bodies);
Fuel cell technology;

Battery management systems for "new energy vehicles";
Automotive accessories;

After-market products (that meet legislative guidelines for vehicle modifications)

Opportunities

In 2010, 18.06 million vehicles were sold in China. Much of this growth still comes from stimulus policies for this industry, especially a tax rebate for cars of 1.6 liters or less and other subsidies for buyers in the countryside.
The obvious trend is that small cars will be popular due to policy guidance and market demand. The Chinese government has promised to reduce the country's carbon emissions dramatically, so more and more policies favor small cars. Meanwhile, after more than 10 years of rapid development, first-tier cities like Beijing, Guangzhou and Shanghai have enormous numbers of cars on the road, so people in second-tier cities will represent the largest potential buyer for the next 10 years, but these buyers are more sensitive to price and so small cars will continue to be popular in second-tier cities.

Another new trend is for Chinese auto companies to purchase overseas automotive companies for brands and technology: BeiQi purchased SAAB and Geely Motors purchased Volvo. That happened partly because Chinese auto manufacturers have accumulated enough money to do this, and partly because they have reached a bottleneck in their business expansion and technology improvement. China exports relatively little in the automotive arena, mostly to African and Latin American countries, but Chinese automakers already have their eye on the U.S. and European markets.

The priority goal for Chinese automotive components, parts, and accessory manufacturers is to improve technology, quality and design capability. Currently, a consortium is working on developing a Chinese automatic transmission, a technology that has eluded them so far. Most of the domestic automotive parts manufacturers' R&D capabilities are limited, due to the small scale of their operations and a shortage of capital to invest in that capability, as compared to international companies. Lately, Chinese companies are dominating the low-end components market and have aggressively sold their parts to U.S. automakers. In the next five years, the Chinese Government will continue to encourage foreign investment in automotive component development and manufacturing, so in the meantime, there is still a market for imports and American products are generally highly regarded by Chinese customers.

However, the opportunity to sell components or parts directly from the U.S. is rapidly diminishing. Most foreign companies have found they need to set up operations in China to sell into the Chinese supply chain. Many U.S. companies have integrated successfully and see a bright future as they expand along with the market.

Recently, the Chinese government launched the "National Project for Electric Vehicles," that encourages the development of environmentally friendly automobiles. U.S. companies possessing clean energy parts and technologies will find more and more opportunities in the Chinese market.

Additionally, as China's restrictions on trading and distribution have been reduced over the years, American companies are gaining the right to distribute most of their own products, including automobiles and related parts, within China. Car dealerships are also about to embark on the business of buying back and selling used cars, although imported used cars continue to be prohibited.

Healthcare Market

Overview

Medical Devices
Unit: USD billion

	2009	2010 (est.)	2011 (forecast)	2012 (forecast)
Total Market Size	$13.9	$15.8	$17.9	$20.4
% y-o-y	17.3%	13.2%	13.8%	13.8%

China is the world's third largest market for medical equipment and is expected to become the second largest market in the next few years. China's medical devices market has been growing steadily fueled by increasing demand for medical equipment, a rapidly aging population, and the stimulation and implementation of China's healthcare reform. Estimates are that over 20,000 hospitals and 30,000 county-level hospitals need to upgrade equipment.

According to BMI, China's medical equipment market will continue to grow at 13-14% annually during the next few years. Total market size was over USD 13.9 billion in 2009 and is estimated to be almost USD16 billion in 2010. Forecasts indicate the market will reach USD 26.8 billion by 2014. Among international suppliers, U.S. companies occupy the largest market share with approximately 35%, followed by Germany and Japan.

Chinese end users consider U.S. products to be of superior quality and the most technologically advanced. China's hospitals particularly welcome medical equipment and products with high-technology content. At the same time, domestic medical device companies are consolidating, upgrading quality, and beginning to compete in medium-level technology niches against international suppliers. Government agencies with procurement authority are subject to budget limits, causing marked price competition among domestic and foreign suppliers. Consequently, foreign suppliers with a good strategy and reasonable price will have better success in China.

According to 2009 estimates, expenditures on medical equipment procurement by central and local-level governments were over RMB100 billion. Currently, the government is investing RMB850 billion in basic hospital infrastructure to guarantee each county to have a minimum of one hospital with a goal of providing basic healthcare access and coverage for the entire population in China. Given the Ministry of Health's focus on rural healthcare, many large global companies have already started readjusting their strategy in China to take advantage of the market and meet these challenges.

Imported medical devices still face challenges centered around the uncertain regulatory environment, extensive delays in registration and re-registration of products, price controls by the central government, and the centralized tendering and procurement process.

Sub-Sector Best Prospects

Best selling prospects in the healthcare sector include:
In-vitro diagnostic equipment and reagents:

Clinical and diagnostic analysis equipment, diagnostic reagents, medical tests and basic equipment/instruments
Implantable and intervention materials and artificial organs:
Intervention materials, implantable artificial organs, contact artificial organs, stents, implantable materials, and artificial organ assisting equipment.

Therapeutic products:
Tri-dimensional Ultrasonic-focused therapeutic systems, body rotary Gamma knives, simulators, linear accelerators, laser diagnostic and surgery equipment, nuclide treatment equipment, physical and rehabilitation equipment.

Medical diagnostic and imaging equipment:
Black/ white and color ultrasonic diagnostic units, sleeping monitors, digital X-ray systems, MRIs, CTs, DRs, and other ultrasound equipment.

Surgery & emergency appliances:
>Anesthesia ventilation systems and components: high-frequency surgery equipment, high-frequency and voltage generators.

Healthcare Information technology related equipment and products:
>Medical software, computer-aided diagnostic equipment, and hospital information systems (HIS, CIS, HLT).

Medical equipment parts and accessories

Travel and Tourism Sector

Overview

According to the Office of Travel & Tourism within the U.S. Department of Commerce, between 2009 and 2015 the number of Chinese travelers to the United States will increase by 346%. Each Chinese tourist spends, on average, about US$3,000 per trip. The high growth rate and contribution to the U.S. economy makes China's outbound tourism market a key component of President Obama's National Export Initiative, which seeks to double U.S. exports by 2015.

American tour operators, Destination Marketing Organizations, hotels and airlines will need to cooperate with each other, as well as with government entities, in order to capture more of this highly profitable market.

Unit: (as noted)

	2009 (estimated)	2010 (estimated)	2011 (forecast)	2012 (forecast)
Total Chinese Outbound Travelers; all destinations (in thousands)	49,702	56,486	64,192	72,473
Chinese Outbound Travelers to the U.S. (in thousands)	525	735	911	1,093
Total International Travelers to China; all countries (in thousands)	49,969	53,832	57,559	61,883

Total expenditures by Chinese Outbound travelers; all destinations (in US$ millions)	45,495	51,714	62,332	73,512
Total receipts by International Travelers to China (in US$ millions)	39,675	44,940	50,113	54,801

Sources: The Economist Intelligence Unit, 2010; Office of Travel & Tourism Industries (USDOC/ITA/MAS)
Total Market Size = 72,473,000 Chinese outbound travelers (2012 forecast)
Data Sources: The Economist Intelligence Unit, 2010
Business Monitor International, "China Tourism Report Q4 2010"
U.S. Department of Commerce > International Trade Administration > Manufacturing & Services > Office of Travel & Tourism Industries

Historically, the Central Government in China restricted where its citizens could travel abroad. In 2000, the number of countries that a Chinese tourist could visit was just 17. By 2009, that number had risen to 138 countries. In 2007, the United States and China signed a Memorandum of Understanding (MOU) to facilitate outbound group travel from China to the U.S., and the MOU has been expanded twice to include more Chinese outbound travel agents.

Corporation for Travel Promotion

On September 10, 2010, U.S. Commerce Secretary Gary Locke appointed 11 travel and tourism industry leaders to serve on the Corporation for Travel Promotion (CTP) Board of Directors. The CTP is a new non-profit corporation that will promote travel to the United States and communicate and improve the entry process so that visitors will want to return.

CTP will help enhance the competitiveness of an already robust industry, which supports more than 8 million American jobs and is a critical source of export strength. Many other nations operate ministries of tourism that actively market their countries as tourist destinations around the world, (i.e. "China National Tourism Administration" or CNTA). CTP will help better market the United States as a destination and encourage people across the globe to travel to the United States.

The Travel Promotion Act of 2009 created the CTP to develop and execute a plan to (a) provide useful information to those interested in traveling to the United States; (b) identify and address perceptions regarding U.S. entry policies; (c) maximize the economic and diplomatic benefits of travel to the United States through the use of various promotional tools; and (d) ensure that international travel benefits all states and the District of Columbia.

Agricultural Sectors

Overview

The United States Department of Agriculture, through the Foreign Agricultural Service (FAS), operates six offices in the People's Republic of China for the purpose of expanding exports of U.S. agriculture, fishery, and forestry products. U.S. agricultural, fishery, and forestry exports to China from January to November 2010 were over USD16 billion, up thirty-eight percent from the same period in 2009, setting a new record for the highest level in history. China is now the second-largest U.S. overseas market for agricultural, fish, and forestry exports. Given China's rising incomes and demand for raw materials and finished foodstuffs, FAS forecasts that China's imports will continue to grow well into the future.

Due to the changing regulatory environment in China, U.S. exporters are advised to carefully check the import regulations. Individuals and enterprises interested in exporting U.S. agricultural, fishery, and forestry commodities to China should contact the FAS offices (listed below) as well as USDA Cooperator organizations. Exporters of U.S. commodities should also review the FAS website (www.fas.usda.gov), which features general information about trade shows and other promotional venues to showcase agricultural products, FAS-sponsored promotional efforts, export financing and assistance, and a directory of registered suppliers and buyers of agricultural, fishery, and forestry goods in the United States and abroad.

Agricultural Sectors
Soybeans
Cotton
Hides and Skins
Corn
Fish and Fish Products
Tobacco
Wood and Wood Products

Market Entry Strategy

The U.S. Embassy and the U.S. Department of Commerce welcome contact with American companies to initiate or expand exports into the China market. Two of the primary objectives of U.S. policy with regard to China are (a) creating jobs and growing the American economy by increasing exports, and (b) ensuring our companies' ability to compete on a level playing field. A company should visit China in order to gain a better perspective and understanding of its potential market and location. Especially given China's rapidly changing market and large area, a visit to China can provide a company great insight into the country, the business climate, and its people. Chinese companies respect "face-to-face" meetings, which can demonstrate a U.S. company's commitment to working in China. Prospective exporters should note that China has many different regions and that each province has unique economic and social characteristics.

Continued long-term relationships are key to finding a good partner in China. To maximize their contacts, companies should aim at forming a network of relationships with people at various levels across a broad range of organizations.

U.S. companies commonly use agents in China to initially create these relationships. Localized agents possess the knowledge and contacts to better promote U.S. products and break down institutional, language, and cultural barriers. The U.S. Commercial Service China offers a wide array of services to assist U.S. exporters in finding Chinese partners through a network of five Commercial Service posts in China. They also have a partnership with the China Council for the Promotion of International Trade (CCPIT) to provide services in 14 other major cities in China. U.S. companies are strongly encouraged to carefully choose potential Chinese partners and take the time to understand their distributors, customers, suppliers, and advisors.

China is a challenging market and requires a strong understanding of a firm's capabilities and in-depth knowledge of the market. Before making a decision to enter the China market, potential exporters should consider their own resources, their past exporting experience, and their willingness to commit a significant amount of time to exploring opportunities for their products and services in China. The U.S. Commercial Service has developed a toolkit to help exporters understand some of these challenges; our "Are You China Ready" assessment is available here.

Regional Information

China's market is geographically diverse with each region full of unique opportunities as well as posing different challenges.

Second-Tier Cities and American Trading Centers:
14 of China's up-and-coming markets are referred to as American Trading Centers (ATCs). These ATCs—from Harbin in the north to Zhuhai in the south—account for 54 percent of the country's imports and are growing at an average rate of 11 percent.

Take advantage of opportunities and export assistance in these growing markets:

• Dalian	• Nanjing	• Wuhan
• Chongqing	• Ningbo	• Xiamen
• Hangzhou	• Qingdao	• Xi'an
• Harbin	• Shenzhen	• Zhuhai
• Kunming	• Tianjin	

Trade Policy Initiatives
Policy Specific Help
The Department of Commerce's International Trade Administration works to ensure that foreign countries, including China, live up to their trade commitments under the WTO and other international trade-related agreements and that trade barriers do not impede the flow of goods and services between the U.S. and foreign markets.

Making sure that foreign markets are open to American businesses and workers, and assisting companies facing export problems overseas is the work of:
Office of China: helping U.S. companies overcome market barriers to doing business in China;

Trade Compliance Center (TCC): ensuring that China's trade agreement obligations to the United States are closely monitored, that compliance violations are addressed promptly, and that U.S. exporters are aware of the rights created by these trade agreements; and

IPR Office: working with U.S. companies to protect and enforce their intellectual property rights in China

Joint Commission on Commerce and Trade (JCCT)

JCCT is the Commerce Department's leading, annual forum for high-level policy dialog with China, utilizing a number of Working Groups and reporting productive Outcomes. Other important policy dialog forums include the U.S.-China Strategic and Economic Dialog (S&ED), led by the Department of Treasury and Department of State.

Risk Management

Doing business in any foreign country can be challenging where incorrect decisions or oversight can pose serious consequences to a company. It is important to recognize the unique risks associated with any specific country and how best to manage these. We can help to take the confusion out of international business and advise companies how best to protect themselves.

Intellectual Property Rights (IPR)

The growing number of pirated and counterfeit goods being distributed internationally threatens America's innovation economy. Products that typically fall prey to these acts include: CDs, DVDs, software, watches, electronic equipment, clothing, processed foods, consumer products, as well as auto parts..

Due Diligence

Verifying credit worthiness and other important information about the business structure and operations of a potential partner, representative or customer is an important step in ensuring success. Prevent costly mistakes with quick, low-cost credit checks or due diligence reports on companies in China

Scams

In China scams take on many forms from requests for upfront payments to cash requested for hosting a banquet in which the cost far exceeds the normal amount. In general if it sounds to be good to be true, it probably is.

Accounting, Auditing and Tax Services

Dezan Shira & Associates
Contact: Sabrina Zhang, Regional Partner
Suite 701, East Tower, Twin Towers,
B-12, Jianguomenwai Avenue,
Chaoyang District, Beijing,100022
Phone: (86) 10 - 6566 0088
Fax: (86) 10 - 6566 0288
Web: www.dezshira.com

Dezan Shira & Associates is a specialist foreign direct investment practice, providing legal, accounting and tax services to multinationals investing in China, Hong Kong, India and Vietnam. Established in 1992, the firm is a leading Asia regional practice with sixteen offices in four jurisdictions, employing over 170 legal, accounting, tax and audit professionals. DSA provides a combination of both legal and tax services to their clients, giving them the ability to acquire professional knowledge in the local legal regulatory environment in each country as well as the tax and financial implications of doing so.

Klako Group
Contact: Sven Koehler, Group Managing Director
1506 Cross Tower, 318 Fuzhou Road, Shanghai
Phone: (86) 21 - 6391 3188
Fax: (86) 21 - 6391 2032
Web: http://www.klakogroup.com

Klako Group is an international accounting and consulting firm established since 1979. Klako Group provides a wide range of market entry consulting, incorporation, tax, audit, accounting and human resource services to organizations currently operating or looking to operate throughout China, Hong Kong, Singapore and other major offshore jurisdictions.

Klako Group is managed by an international and local team of over 100 certified public accountants, legal and professional consultants who work in our 10 offices in China, Hong Kong and Singapore. Klako Group has 4 affiliate offices in the US.

US-Pacific Rim International, Inc.
Contact: Anthony Goh, President
Room 1105, Building C, Huapu Garden, 9 Dongzhimen South
Street, Dongcheng District
Beijing, 100007 China
Phone: 86-10-8447-7768/7173
Fax: 86-10-8447-7758
Web: http://www.us-pacific-rim.com

USPRI assists foreign companies market and sell their products, technologies, and services in China. Our signature service is the ChinaOffice Program, through which we establish a team of sales and technical professionals to manage and execute marketing and sales on behalf of our clients. By serving as our client's all-in-one office in China, not only we can serve as their on-the-ground support, but we can save them the tens of thousands of dollars it costs to open their own office, find their own talent search agency, hire accountants, and navigate the Chinese legal system.

Wright & Kou Trust & Finance Advisory, Ltd.
Contact: William Wright, Attorney
Full Tower Suite 908
9 East Third Ring Road, Chaoyang District
Beijing 100020 China
Phone: (86-10)8591-0295
Fax: (86-10)8591-0297
Email: wwright@wrightandkou.com

Our licensed company provides a full range of accounting and tax-filing services, and enterprise management services, to take the hassle out of local compliance for foreign companies and individuals. Our specialties include rep office and WFOE setup and closure, expat personal tax filing, and annual inspections.

Banking and Financial services

City National Bank
Contact: Thomas J. Burr, SVP/Manager - Export Finance
32/F, Kerry Centre 1515 Nanjing Road West Shanghai 200040
P.R.C.
Phone: (888) 488-9700
Email: Thomas.Burr@cnb.com
Web: http://www.cnb.com/business/international/

City National Bank serves successful companies that are global or ready to go global. Established in 1954, City National Bank is a Moody's AA-rated financial institution, placing it in the top 1 percent of all US banks. City National provides working capital loans for export finance, international banking, letters of credit services, and foreign exchange. Its powerful team of experts and its relationships with the Ex-Im Bank, the U.S. Commercial Service, and the Bank of East Asia as well as other foreign banks uniquely qualify City National Bank to help its clients export their products to the world. City National Bank member FDIC.

Comerica Bank
Contact: Gigi R. Moore, Senior Vice President
1336 Huashan Rd, 10A3, Shanghai, 200052 China
Phone: 313.222.7031
Email: gmoore@comerica.com
Web: http://www.comerica.com

Comerica Bank is a subsidiary of Comerica Incorporated, which has assets in excess of $67 billion and is headquartered in Dallas, TX. In addition to Texas, Comerica Bank locations can be found in Arizona, California, Florida and Michigan, with select businesses operating in several other states, as well as in Canada, China and Mexico. Comerica Bank offers a broad array of financial services, including export and import solutions that support every stage of the global supply chain, with solutions to optimize working capital, mitigate risks and simplify the trade process. Comerica Bank is a Super Delegated Authority and the Fast Track lender for the Ex-Im Bank Working Capital Guarantee Program.

PNC Financial Services Group
Contact: Alan Andrews, Vice President, Global Treasury
Contact: David.Zhang,
Phone: 412-768-7662
Fax: 412-762-5022
Email: david_zhang@gvlocalization.com
Web: http://www.pncbank.com/tradefinance

Headquartered in Pittsburgh PA, PNC Bank, National Association (PNC) is a member of The PNC Financial Services Group, Inc., one of the largest diversified financial services organizations in the United States. For over 30 years, PNC has supported importers located outside of the U.S. by financing the purchase of machinery, equipment or services from American suppliers.
Consistently a top user of Ex-Im Bank programs (by number of transactions), PNC has helped hundreds of companies in many countries to meet their financing needs and realize their business goals. In addition to short and medium-term financing programs, PNC offers a wide range of international banking services including letters of credit, documentary collections, bankers' acceptances, foreign exchange and derivatives trading, international cash management, and correspondent banking.

TD Bank
Contact: Margaret Carolan, VP/International Trade Services
6000 Atrium Way
Mount Laurel, NJ 08054
Phone: 1-800-751-9000 Ext. 6554
Email: mcarolan@yesbank.com
Web: http://www.commerceonline.com

Following TD Bank Financial Group's acquisition of Commerce Bancorp Inc. on March 31, 2008, TD Banknorth and Commerce Bank merged on May 31, 2008, to be known as TD Bank, America's Most Convenient Bank. Today, TD Banknorth and Commerce Bank form one of the 20 largest commercial banking organizations in the United States with over $114 billion in assets, and provide customers with a full range of financial products and services at nearly 1,100 convenient locations from Maine to Florida. Commerce Bank is headquartered in Cherry Hill, NJ. TD Banknorth and Commerce Bank are trade names of

TD Bank, N.A. For more information, visit www.TDBanknorth.com and www.commerceonline.com.

Business Administration Services

US-Pacific Rim International, Inc.
Contact: Anthony Goh, President
Room 1105, Building C, Huapu Garden, 9 Dongzhimen South
Street, Dongcheng District
Beijing, 100007 China
Phone: 86-10-8447-7768/7173
Fax: 86-10-8447-7758
Email: anthony.goh@us-pacific-rim.com
Web: http://www.us-pacific-rim.com

USPRI assists foreign companies market and sell their products, technologies, and services in China. Our signature service is the ChinaOffice Program, through which we establish a team of sales and technical professionals to manage and execute marketing and sales on behalf of our clients. By serving as our client's all-in-one office in China, not only we can serve as their on-the-ground support, but we can save them the tens of thousands of dollars it costs to open their own office, find their own talent search agency, hire accountants, and navigate the Chinese legal system.

Business Consulting

CTR Market Research Co., LTD.
Contact: Chase Kusterer, Client Manager
4/F Yunhai Yuan, No.118 Qinghai Road
Shanghai, China 200041
Phone: (+86) 021-6271-7766 *520
Fax: (+86) 021-5228-1880
Email: chase_kusterer@ctrchina.cn
Web: http://www.ctrchina.cn

China's largest market information and insight provider. Founded as a joint venture company between CITVC and Kantar Group.
As the market leading provider, we integrate local expertise with cutting-edge research technology and innovative thinking to meet clients' needs for 360° media intelligence services.
Our strategic goal is to be the preferred research partner and market leader in delivering value-added marketing information and insights to help our clients make more effective decisions.

China Sage Consultants (Shanghai) Co., Ltd Contact: Chris Wingo, Managing Director
Jing'An District, 829 Yan'An Middle Road, West Tower 10-C, Shanghai 200040
Phone: +1 (714) 656-3488
Email: inquire@ChinaSageConsultants.com
Web: http://www.ChinaSageConsultants.com

China Sage Consultants has been delivering US SME-size companies sustainable sales in China since 2003. Our sales programs provide everything needed to sell, market and build-up your long-term presence in China. We make having your own sales team in China an economical, low-risk and high-results proposition. With years of accumulated B2B China sales and business experience, we will ensure your foray into China is a successful one. Client companies range in size from $5M to $250M+ in global sales. Are you ready for China and how fast can we start - Contact us to learn more. American owned and managed.

China Solutions LLC

Contact: Nestor Gounaris, Managing Partner
Room 1027, Building 8, No. 1147, Kangding Road,Jing'an
District, Shanghai 200040
Phone: 86 21 6471 0499
Fax: +1 631 251 6984
Email: ngounaris@chinasolutionsllc.com
Web: http://www.chinasolutionsllc.com

China Solutions leverages more than 20 years of in-country experience to deliver legal and operational solutions needed to efficiently and effectively achieve commercial objectives. We facilitate and assist with foreign direct investment and corresponding matters, including due diligence, negotiations and documentation, approvals and registrations, regulatory compliance and applications, research, bi-lingual document preparation, labor advice, corporate restructuring, and high value-added solutions. Our comprehensive, professional, and reliable approach and our deep and broad range of experience allow us to effectively advise our clients to achieve their objectives in China.

ChinaGate Company Limited

Contact: Xiajing Chen, New Business Development Director
Unit 1505-1506, Orient Center, 699 Nanjing West Road,
Shanghai 200041, China
Phone: (86 21) 5211-0772
Fax: (86 21) 5211-0317
Email: danny.chen@chinagateco.com
Web: http://www.chinagate-healthcare.com
http://www.optum.com

ChinaGate is now OPTUMInsight, part of Optum-a leading health services business.ChinaGate is a high-quality specialty Consumer Healthcare consulting company focus on providing complete regulatory service in China. Our qualified professional experienced consultants are well versed in government regulations that cover products in Drug, medical Devices, IVDs, Cosmetics, Health Food categories. Our Affiliated Network includes partners in China for Marketing & Sales, Market Research, Legal, Distribution and HR training as well as global partnership with western international companies.

Chinapex

Contact: James Wang, Engagement Manager
Chinapex USA Office, 111 Deerwood Rd, San Ramon, CA
94583
Phone: 1-925-203-5700
Fax: 1-925-226-2437
Email: james.wang@chinapex.com
Web: http://www.chinapex.com

Chinapex is a full-service market expansion firm that helps companies enter China and accelerate revenue growth with low risk and cost-effectiveness. We provide our clients a comprehensive solution that includes strategy and insight as well on-ground implementation and operations.
Our services include research & consulting, market development (sales & marketing), business operations support, and sourcing. Our robust solutions and empower companies in all stages of China market development.

Dezan Shira & Associates

Contact: Sabrina Zhang, Regional Partner
Suite 701, East Tower, Twin Towers,
B-12, Jianguomenwai Avenue,
Chaoyang District, Beijing,100022
Phone: (86) 10 - 6566 0088
Fax: (86) 10 - 6566 0288
Email: Sabrina.zhang@dezshira.com
Web: http://www.dezshira.com

Dezan Shira & Associates is a specialist foreign direct investment practice, providing legal, accounting and tax services to multinationals investing in China, Hong Kong, India and Vietnam. Established in 1992, the firm is a leading Asia regional practice with sixteen offices in four jurisdictions, employing over 170 legal, accounting, tax and audit professionals. DSA provides a combination of both legal and tax services to their clients, giving them the ability to acquire professional knowledge in the local legal regulatory environment in each country as well as the tax and financial implications of doing so.

Hill & Associates

Contact: Iain Young, Business Development Director
6A Huamin Empire Plaza, 728 Yanan Xi Road, Shanghai, China

Phone: (86) 21 - 5238 5599
Fax: (86) 21 - 5237 1693
Email: iain.young@hill-assoc.com
Web: http://www.hill-assoc.com

Hill & Associates, a G4S company, is a globally recognized leader in enterprise risk management with a long and successful track record in China and the AP Region from Japan to Pakistan. We operate in 4 primary business units:
Fraud Prevention and Integrity Risk Consulting and Advisory, Corporate Intelligence, Risk Management/Protective Security and Risk Intelligence.

InsightChina
Contact: Garry Chen, Managing Director
18D North Yintong Plaza, 1016 Dingxi Road, Changning District, Shanghai, PRC
Phone: (86) 21 - 6251-0138
Fax: (86) 21 - 6251-5700
Email: Garry@Insight-China.com
Web: http://www.insight-china.com
InsightChina is a professional business consulting firm based in Shanghai. We specialize in helping you navigate the many complexities of the Chinese market. Our 20 plus years of business management experience in China, combined with our unique understanding of both Chinese and Western cultures and business environments allows us to create and implement tailor-made solutions to ensure your success.
InsightChina can assist you with the following:
·Market Research
·Business Planning & Strategy
·Company Setup
·Partner Search
·Business Management
·HR Management & Recruitment

REACH24H CONSULTING GROUP
Contact: NATHAN CHEN, Deputy General Manager
6th Floor, Building No.2, Hopson Center, No 327 Tianmushan Rd
Hangzhou Zhejiang, 310023 China
Phone: 86 13185024868
Fax: 86 13185024868

Email: nathan.chen@reach24h.ccom
Web: https://www.reach24h.com

REACH24H Group provides product Stewardship & regulatory compliance service for global customers from its three offices – Ireland, Canada and China, assisting global companies to comply with global chemical regulations including the EU REACH, China new chemical substance notification, Global GHS, USA TSCA, etc.

Sunfaith China Ltd.
Contact: Kevin Sun, President
28th Floor, Tower B Eton Plaza, No.555 Pudong Avenue
Shanghai, 200120
Phone: 86-21-61682616
Fax: +86-21-61682956
Email: kevin_sun@sunfaith.com
Web: www.sunfaith.com

Sunfaith is the trusted advisor dedicated to help its clients protect and enhance enterprise value in China. Our 3 core businesses are brand protection and anti-counterfeiting (give one stop solutions to intellectual property infringement issue to clients), market and competitive intelligence (help clients to better understand and act on the market, regulation and competitive status in China) and corporate investigation (to reduce business risks raised by improper internal control).

The JLJ Group
Contact: Timothy Lamb, Director
Suite 603-605, Oriental Center 699 Nanjing West Rd. / 31
Wujiang Rd. Shanghai 200041 China
Phone: 021-52110787
Fax: 021-52110069
Email: tim.lamb@jljgroup.com
Web: http://www.jljgroup.com

The JLJ Group is a one-stop service provider assisting international companies in their mission to enter and grow in the China market. JLJ combines the expertise of in-house specialists to provide services critical to our clients' China operations, including: Market Research & Consulting, Corporate Formation, Accounting, Recruitment, and Payroll & HR Outsourcing.

Since 1995, we have assisted more than 500 clients from over 30 countries, ranging from Fortune 500 to small and medium sized enterprises, as well as government organizations. Our offices are located in Shanghai, Beijing, Boston (US), and Milan (Italy).

US-Pacific Rim International, Inc.
Contact: Anthony Goh, President
Room 1105, Building C, Huapu Garden, 9 Dongzhimen South Street, Dongcheng District
Beijing, 100007 China
Phone: 86-10-8447-7768/7173
Fax: 86-10-8447-7758
Email: anthony.goh@us-pacific-rim.com
Web: http://www.us-pacific-rim.com

USPRI assists foreign companies market and sell their products, technologies, and services in China. Our signature service is the ChinaOffice Program, through which we establish a team of sales and technical professionals to manage and execute marketing and sales on behalf of our clients. By serving as our client's all-in-one office in China, not only we can serve as their on-the-ground support, but we can save them the tens of thousands of dollars it costs to open their own office, find their own talent search agency, hire accountants, and navigate the Chinese legal system.

Wang & Partners
Contact: Nicole Wang, Partner
Room 0806, Tower A2, Da Cheng International Center, No. 78, Dong Si Huan Zhong Road, Chaoyang District, Beijing, P.R.China (P.C.:100124)
Phone: +86-10-5979 2078 ext. 8002
Fax: +86-10-5962 5974
Email: law@wangandpartners.com
Web: http://www.wangandpartners.com

A member of the International Trademark Association since its inception, Wang and Partners is a Chinese owned and operated Intellectual Property law firm. Expert knowledge of local laws and systems, and a cross cultural approach will legally protect your business in China. Bring your business to China the Chinese way.

Business Development

BEIJING KUNRONG LAW FIRM
Contact: Yi Sun, Partner
1521, Block A, Boya International Center,
No.1 Lizezhongyi Road,
Chaoyang District, Beijing, China
Phone: (86) 10 - 8478 2027-803/802/801, 10 - 5718 7871
Fax: (86) 10 - 8478 2027-808
Email: sun28564@163.com
Web: http://www.95lawyer.com

Beijing Kun Rong lawfirm has developed wide-ranging contacts and experience in all sectors of China practice and has dealt with projects throughout China for a diverse cross-section of clients.
Scope of key services:
Foreign Direct Investment; Set up of Representative Offices and Branches; Company Formation; Taxation; Intellectual Property; Corporate Finance; Merger and Acquisition; Listing Banking; Due diligence; Litigation and Arbitration
Verification and Attestation of Legal Documents; USA and Canada visa.

China Sage Consultants (Shanghai) Co., Ltd Contact: Chris Wingo, Managing Director
Jing'An District, 829 Yan'An Middle Road, West Tower 10-C, Shanghai 200040
Phone: +1 (714) 656-3488
Email: inquire@ChinaSageConsultants.com
Web: http://www.ChinaSageConsultants.com

China Sage Consultants has been delivering US SME-size companies sustainable sales in China since 2003. Our sales programs provide everything needed to sell, market and build-up your long-term presence in China. We make having your own sales team in China an economical, low-risk and high-results proposition. With years of accumulated B2B China sales and business experience, we will ensure your foray into China is a successful one. Client companies range in size from $5M to $250M+ in global sales. Are you ready for China and how fast can we start - Contact us to learn more. American owned and managed.

Chinapex
Contact: James Wang, Engagement Manager
Chinapex USA Office, 111 Deerwood Rd, San Ramon, CA 94583
Phone: 1-925-203-5700
Fax: 1-925-226-2437
Email: james.wang@chinapex.com
Web: http://www.chinapex.com

Chinapex is a full-service market expansion firm that helps companies enter China and accelerate revenue growth with low risk and cost-effectiveness. We provide our clients a comprehensive solution that includes strategy and insight as well on-ground implementation and operations.
Our services include research & consulting, market development (sales & marketing), business operations support, and sourcing. Our robust solutions and empower companies in all stages of China market development.

Diversified Trade Company, LLC
Contact: Stephanie Summers-Farr, CEO
6340 Sugarloaf Parkway Suite 200
Duluth Georgia, 30097 United States
Phone: 601-353-2522
Fax: 601-519-4093
Email: stephanie@diversifiedtradecompany.com
Web: http://www.diversifiedtradecompany.com

Since 1998, Diversified Trade Company, LLC has been assisting U.S and foreign companies to increase their market share into other countries. Using our most precious resource, our relationships, DTC provides market research, export/ import management, buyer identification, contract negotiation, product pricing and project management services.

US-Pacific Rim International, Inc.
Contact: Anthony Goh, President
Room 1105, Building C, Huapu Garden, 9 Dongzhimen South Street, Dongcheng District

Beijing, 100007 China
Phone: 86-10-8447-7768/7173
Fax: 86-10-8447-7758
Email: anthony.goh@us-pacific-rim.com
Web: http://www.us-pacific-rim.com

USPRI assists foreign companies market and sell their products, technologies, and services in China. Our signature service is the ChinaOffice Program, through which we establish a team of sales and technical professionals to manage and execute marketing and sales on behalf of our clients. By serving as our client's all-in-one office in China, not only we can serve as their on-the-ground support, but we can save them the tens of thousands of dollars it costs to open their own office, find their own talent search agency, hire accountants, and navigate the Chinese legal system.

Universal Consensus
Contact: Denise Pirrotti Hummel, CEO
2173 Salk Ave. Suite 250
Carlsbad CA, 92008 United States
Phone: +1(760)696-0151
Email: info@universalconsensus.com
Web: http://www.universalconsensus.com

Cultural differences may be the biggest obstacle to success in China. Universal Consensus helps companies with strategic consulting and training to overcome cultural differences, turning challenges into opportunities.
Our proprietary Business Model of Intercultural Analysis (BMIA) is a tool for driving profit and reducing risk in foreign markets. On average, we have helped clients grow sales in China by 25%. Other clients include Whirlpool, Qualcomm, the U.S. State Department and the U.S. Department of Defense.

Customs Brokerage

Beijing China Consultants Freight Forwarding Co.,Ltd
Shanghai Branch
Contact: Lili Wu, Sales Manager
Room 1201,Block C of the Hongkou District Hua Changlu No. 9
as building Shanghai,China 100025
Phone: 0086-021-55570281
Fax: 0086-021-66286068
Email: lili.wu@bccff-sh.com
Web: http://www.bccff-sh.com

BCCFF-Shanghai Branch is one part of BCCFF that is the class-A forwarding company. We provides professional service for ocean shipping, air parcel, sea air combined transport, declare at the customs、 freight forwarder of SCM. We can provide the impartial, professional and individual service base on we are full of service experience for 11 years. Our management includes traditional Chinese culture and Scientific operation skill.

Distributors, Sales Agents and Importers

China MedConnect LLC
Contact: Landon Lack, President and CEO
Bldg 4-2-62 Jianguomenwai Diplomatic Compound
Beijing, 100600
Phone: +86-139-1130-8164
Email: landon.lack@chinamedconnect.net
Web: www.chinamedconnect.net

China MedConnect represents US medical device companies with their operations and interests in mainland China. We are licensed by the China SFDA to act as Registration Agent, Service Agent and Legal Agent for US medical device companies. We support our clients with both market entry and on-the-ground representation. We offer an established and trusted network of medical device distributors, clinical sales and marketing support, sourcing solutions, and investment & strategic advisory services. All of our work is focused exclusively in the US to China medical device community.

US-Pacific Rim International, Inc.
Contact: Anthony Goh, President
Room 1105, Building C, Huapu Garden, 9 Dongzhimen South Street, Dongcheng District
Beijing, 100007 China
Phone: 86-10-8447-7768/7173
Fax: 86-10-8447-7758
Email: anthony.goh@us-pacific-rim.com
Web: http://www.us-pacific-rim.com

USPRI assists foreign companies market and sell their products, technologies, and services in China. Our signature service is the ChinaOffice Program, through which we establish a team of sales and technical professionals to manage and execute marketing and sales on behalf of our clients. By serving as our client's all-in-one office in China, not only we can serve as their on-the-ground support, but we can save them the tens of thousands of dollars it costs to open their own office, find their own talent search agency, hire accountants, and navigate the Chinese legal system.

Education and Training Services

Occam Consulting Limited
Contact: Tony Childs, Director
1203, Building1, Xujiahui Lu, Shanghai
Phone: +86 1381 633 8844
Email: tony@occam.cn
Web: http://www.occam.cn

Occam has deployed over 300 China Business Training courses and counts amongst its clients' over 50 multinational companies & two governments (UK & NZ). Occam products & services are all developed in-house based on market needs & our clients requirements and goals. We have trained business people and government personnel from 30+ countries are based in Shanghai and provide services worldwide. 50% of training participants are Chinese nationals working in foreign companies and 50% are foreigners. Training can be deployed in English or Chinese.

Environmental Services

REACH24H CONSULTING GROUP
Contact: NATHAN CHEN, Deputy General Manager
6th Floor, Building No.2, Hopson Center, No 327 Tianmushan Rd
Hangzhou Zhejiang, 310023 China
Phone: 86 13185024868
Fax: 86 13185024868
Email: nathan.chen@reach24h.ccom
Web: https://www.reach24h.com

REACH24H Group provides product Stewardship & regulatory compliance service for global customers from its three offices – Ireland, Canada and China, assisting global companies to comply with global chemical regulations including the EU REACH, China new chemical substance notification, Global GHS, USA TSCA, etc.

Consultation Co., Ltd.
Contact: Ting Zhu, Director of Business Development
No.865 Hezheng Rd. Jiading District
Shanghai, 201822 China
Phone: +(86 21) 5998 9191
Fax: +(86 21) 5998 9393
Email: zhuting0717@126.com
Web: http://www.shlabor.com/

Shanghai Labor Co. is a leading analytical laboratory for environmental testing services in China. It focuses on providing outstanding testing service, technical expertise, consultation and solution for detection of workplace hazards, hygienic for radiation, drinking water, public place and indoor environment, air and waste gas, water and wastewater and noise.
 Shanghai Labor is holding accreditations from American Industrial Hygiene Association (AIHA) as an accredited Industrial Hygiene laboratory (ID: 198270); China National Accreditation Service for Conformity Assessment (CNAS); and certificates from China Metrology Accreditation and Shanghai Production Safety Supervision and Administration.

Export Management

Diversified Trade Company, LLC
Contact: Stephanie Summers-Farr, CEO
6340 Sugarloaf Parkway Suite 200
Duluth Georgia, 30097 United States
Phone: 601-353-2522
Fax: 601-519-4093
Email: stephanie@diversifiedtradecompany.com
Web: http://www.diversifiedtradecompany.com

Since 1998, Diversified Trade Company, LLC has been assisting U.S and foreign companies to increase their market share into other countries. Using our most precious resource, our relationships, DTC provides market research, export/ import management, buyer identification, contract negotiation, product pricing and project management services.

Hospitals, Clinics and Health Services

ChinaGate Company Limited
Contact: Xiajing Chen, New Business Development Director
Unit 1505-1506, Orient Center, 699 Nanjing West Road,
Shanghai 200041, China
Phone: (86 21) 5211-0772
Fax: (86 21) 5211-0317
Email: danny.chen@chinagateco.com
Web: http://www.chinagate-healthcare.com
http://www.optum.com

ChinaGate is now OPTUMInsight, part of Optum-a leading health services business.ChinaGate is a high-quality specialty Consumer Healthcare consulting company focus on providing complete regulatory service in China. Our qualified professional experienced consultants are well versed in government regulations that cover products in Drug, medical Devices, IVDs, Cosmetics, Health Food categories. Our Affiliated Network includes partners in China for Marketing & Sales, Market Research, Legal, Distribution and HR training as well as global partnership with western international companies.

Legal Services

BEIJING KUNRONG LAW FIRM
Contact: Yi Sun, Partner
1521, Block A, Boya International Center,
No.1 Lizezhongyi Road,
Chaoyang District, Beijing, China
Phone: (86) 10 - 8478 2027-803/802/801, 10 - 5718 7871
Fax: (86) 10 - 8478 2027-808
Email: sun28564@163.com
Web: http://www.95lawyer.com

Beijing Kun Rong lawfirm has developed wide-ranging contacts and experience in all sectors of China practice and has dealt with projects throughout China for a diverse cross-section of clients.
Scope of key services:
Foreign Direct Investment; Set up of Representative Offices and Branches; Company Formation; Taxation; Intellectual Property; Corporate Finance; Merger and Acquisition; Listing Banking; Due diligence; Litigation and Arbitration
Verification and Attestation of Legal Documents; USA and Canada visa.

Baker & McKenzie
Contact: Lothar Determann, Partner
8th Floor, Henley Building 5 Queens Road Central, Hong Kong
Phone: (415) 576-3000
Email: lothar.determann@bakernet.com
Web: http://www.bakernet.com

Baker & McKenzie has provided sophisticated legal advice and services to many of the world's most dynamic and global organizations for more than 50 years. We are a law firm of more than 3,600 locally qualified, internationally experienced lawyers in 38 countries, we have the knowledge and resources to deliver the broad scope of quality legal services required to respond effectively to both international and local needs - consistently, confidently and with sensitivity for cultural, social and legal practice differences. The more than 10,000 lawyers, supporting professionals and staff of Baker & McKenzie share common values of integrity, personal responsibility and tenacity in an enthusiastic client service culture.

China Solutions LLC
Contact: Nestor Gounaris, Managing Partner
Room 1027, Building 8, No. 1147, Kangding Road,Jing'an District, Shanghai 200040
Phone: 86 21 6471 0499
Fax: +1 631 251 6984
Email: ngounaris@chinasolutionsllc.com
Web: http://www.chinasolutionsllc.com

China Solutions leverages more than 20 years of in-country experience to deliver legal and operational solutions needed to efficiently and effectively achieve commercial objectives. We facilitate and assist with foreign direct investment and corresponding matters, including due diligence, negotiations and documentation, approvals and registrations, regulatory compliance and applications, research, bi-lingual document preparation, labor advice, corporate restructuring, and high value-added solutions. Our comprehensive, professional, and reliable approach and our deep and broad range of experience allow us to effectively advise our clients to achieve their objectives in China.

Dezan Shira & Associates
Contact: Sabrina Zhang, Regional Partner
Suite 701, East Tower, Twin Towers,
B-12, Jianguomenwai Avenue,
Chaoyang District, Beijing,100022
Phone: (86) 10 - 6566 0088
Fax: (86) 10 - 6566 0288
Email: Sabrina.zhang@dezshira.com
Web: http://www.dezshira.com

Dezan Shira & Associates is a specialist foreign direct investment practice, providing legal, accounting and tax services to multinationals investing in China, Hong Kong, India and Vietnam. Established in 1992, the firm is a leading Asia regional practice with sixteen offices in four jurisdictions, employing over 170 legal, accounting, tax and audit professionals. DSA provides a combination of both legal and tax services to their clients, giving them the ability to acquire professional knowledge in the local legal regulatory environment in each country as well as the tax and financial implications of doing so.

Guzov Ofsink, LLC
Contact: Darren Ofsink, Member
900 Third Avenue, 5th Floor
New York, 10022
Phone: 212-371-8008
Fax: 212-688-7273
Email: dofsink@golawintl.com
Web: http://www.golawintl.com

At Guzov Ofsink, LLC ("GO"), our foundation rests on responsiveness, efficiency and innovation and our philosophy starts and ends with our clients, who drive our success. Out of our focus on client service and our reverence for long-term relationships, our practice has grown to meet a wide range of our clients' business and personal needs. Our practice areas have evolved into an international suite of legal services complemented by exemplary assistance to our clients. No matter your location, GO and our extensive international network can assist you.

Juntai Law Firm Shanghai Office
Contact: Li Ni, Lawyer
Suite.602.Huaxia Bank Tower, No. 256 Pudong Road (South)
Fax: 021-63503008
Email: lini@juntailaw.com
Web: http://www.juntailaw.com

Juntai Law Firm (established in 1999) is one of the leading law firms in China with its offices in Beijing, Shanghai, Shenzhen and Nanjing. Currently Juntai has over 180 lawyers nationwide. In 2011, Juntai was awarded as the National Outstanding Law Firm for year 2008-2010 by the China National Bar Association. We are committed to distinguishing ourselves by delivering high quality service to our clients. We learn all that we can about your business and industry so that we can treat you the way you want to be treated individually.

REACH24H CONSULTING GROUP

Contact: NATHAN CHEN, Deputy General Manager
6th Floor, Building No.2, Hopson Center, No 327 Tianmushan Rd
Hangzhou Zhejiang, 310023 China
Phone: 86 13185024868
Fax: 86 13185024868
Email: nathan.chen@reach24h.ccom
Web: https://www.reach24h.com

REACH24H Group provides product Stewardship & regulatory compliance service for global customers from its three offices – Ireland, Canada and China, assisting global companies to comply with global chemical regulations including the EU REACH, China new chemical substance notification, Global GHS, USA TSCA, etc.

Sunfaith China Ltd.
Contact: Kevin Sun, President
28th Floor, Tower B Eton Plaza, No.555 Pudong Avenue
Shanghai, 200120
Phone: 86-21-61682616
Fax: +86-21-61682956
Email: kevin_sun@sunfaith.com
Web: www.sunfaith.com

Sunfaith is the trusted advisor dedicated to help its clients protect and enhance enterprise value in China. Our 3 core businesses are brand protection and anti-counterfeiting (give one stop solutions to intellectual property infringement issue to clients), market and competitive intelligence (help clients to better understand and act on the market, regulation and competitive status in China) and corporate investigation (to reduce business risks raised by improper internal control).

WRIGHT & KOU
Contact: William A. Wright, Attorney
Full Tower Suite 908
9 East Third Ring Road, Chaoyang District
Beijing 100020 China
Phone: (86-10) 8591-0295
Fax: (86-10) 8591-0297
Email: wwright@wrightandkou.com

Wright & Kou's head office is in Beijing's CBD. The firm covers China as a full service law office licensed to practice Chinese law. We provide China corporate, tax, IP, HR, contracts, trade, and litigation services. Mr. Wright is a graduate of Harvard Law School who also holds a doctorate in economics from Oxford University and has 30 years of experience in China. Our clients include a broad range of American and European companies in many manufacturing, agricultural, and service industries.

Wang & Partners

Contact: Nicole Wang, Partner
Room 0806, Tower A2, Da Cheng International Center, No. 78, Dong Si Huan Zhong Road, Chaoyang District, Beijing, P.R.China (P.C.:100124)
Phone: +86-10-5979 2078 ext. 8002
Fax: +86-10-5962 5974
Email: law@wangandpartners.com
Web: http://www.wangandpartners.com

A member of the International Trademark Association since its inception, Wang and Partners is a Chinese owned and operated Intellectual Property law firm. Expert knowledge of local laws and systems, and a cross cultural approach will legally protect your business in China. Bring your business to China the Chinese way.

Manufacturing and Industrial Production Services

China Performance Group
Contact: David De Clercq, Business Development Manager
Presidential Plaza II, Suite 16, 1273 Bound Brook Road
Middlesex New Jersey, 08846 United States
Phone: +1-732-469-8898
Email: info@chinaperformancegroup.com
Web: http://www.chinaperformancegroup.com

China Performance Group is a full sourcing service provider and supply chain advisory firm. With offices in China, the U.S., and Europe, CPG has been helping American companies do business in and with China since 1978, focusing on helping to develop and maintain successful sourcing programs. CPG has developed its know-how through decades of onsite experience cooperating in over 20 industries and 1,000 different product types. During this time, CPG has fine tuned a proprietary system for supply chain management that ensures optimal costs, quality control and timely deliveries for its clients.

Market Research

CTR Market Research Co., LTD.
Contact: Chase Kusterer, Client Manager
4/F Yunhai Yuan, No.118 Qinghai Road
Shanghai, China 200041
Phone: (+86) 021-6271-7766 *520
Fax: (+86) 021-5228-1880
Email: chase_kusterer@ctrchina.cn
Web: http://www.ctrchina.cn

China's largest market information and insight provider. Founded as a joint venture company between CITVC and Kantar Group.
As the market leading provider, we integrate local expertise with cutting-edge research technology and innovative thinking to meet clients' needs for 360° media intelligence services.
Our strategic goal is to be the preferred research partner and market leader in delivering value-added marketing information and insights to help our clients make more effective decisions.

DBSINO Consulting Co., Ltd.
Contact: Roman Luo , Director
905 Shengshi Building A, No.98 Jianguo Lu, Chaoyang District
Beijing, 100022
Phone: 0086-10-85802832
Fax: 0086-10-64000327
Email: Roman@ddsino.com
Web: http://dbsino.com

DBSINO Consulting was established by market research professionals and experts who have at least 8-10 years experiences in Chinese market.
We investigate the domestic macro-market from three levels: industry, company and product.

Marketing, Public Relations and Sales

China Elite Focus Limited
Contact: Pierre Gervois, CEO
Suite 2406 Hopewell Centre, 183 Queen's Road
Hong Kong, China
Phone: +(852)27310602
Fax: +(852)30121522
Email: info@chinaelitefocus.com
Web: http://www.chinaelitefocus.com

China Elite Focus is the leading marketing and PR agency targeting the new generation of affluent & wealthy Chinese outbound tourists interested in luxury travel to the US. We provide very targeted marketing services to reach on-line an audience of high-end Chinese travelers and convince them to choose a hotel, a Travel Agency, a City, a County or a particular State in the US for their next leisure trip.

China Sage Consultants (Shanghai) Co., Ltd.
Contact: Chris Wingo, Managing Director
Jing'An District, 829 Yan'An Middle Road, West Tower 10-C, Shanghai 200040
Phone: +1 (714) 656-3488
Email: inquire@ChinaSageConsultants.com
Web: http://www.ChinaSageConsultants.com

China Sage Consultants has been delivering US SME-size companies sustainable sales in China since 2003. Our sales programs provide everything needed to sell, market and build-up your long-term presence in China. We make having your own sales team in China an economical, low-risk and high-results proposition. With years of accumulated B2B China sales and business experience, we will ensure your foray into China is a successful one. Client companies range in size from $5M to $250M+ in global sales. Are you ready for China and how fast can we start - Contact us to learn more.

Chinapex
Contact: James Wang, Engagement Manager
Chinapex USA Office, 111 Deerwood Rd, San Ramon, CA 94583

Phone: 1-925-203-5700
Fax: 1-925-226-2437
Email: james.wang@chinapex.com
Web: http://www.chinapex.com

Chinapex is a full-service market expansion firm that helps companies enter China and accelerate revenue growth with low risk and cost-effectiveness. We provide our clients a comprehensive solution that includes strategy and insight as well on-ground implementation and operations.
Our services include research & consulting, market development (sales & marketing), business operations support, and sourcing. Our robust solutions and empower companies in all stages of China market development.

WINS Mobile, Inc.
Contact: Sylvia XU, COO
No.7 Alley 251 (Guimei Villa) Guiping Rd., Xuhui District, Shanghai, China (Zip Code: 200233)
Phone: (+86 21) 5407 0958
Email: xuxiao@winsmedia.cn
Web: http://www.winsmob.com

WINSMob is a leading mobile advertising and app development company headquartered in Shanghai, China. The company offers comprehensive mobile solutions from In-App Ads, Mobile Marketing, to Corporate App Development. WINSMob's advanced, proprietary mobile technology and commitment to customer satisfaction are what define them as the most professional mobile advertising platform in China, which supports the vast array of connected devices, and serves many of the world's most renowned brands.

Office Rental

Regus Business Centre
Contact: Andrew Chen, Corporate Account Director
Silver Centre, 1388 North Shaan Xi Road
Shanghai
Phone: +86 (0) 21 6149 8016
Fax: +86 (0) 21 6149 8016
Email: AndrewLu.Chen@regus.com
Web: http://www.regus.cn

Regus is the world's largest provider of workplace solutions. Regus enables people to work their way, whether it's from home, on the road or from an office. Customers such as Google, GlaxoSmithKline, and Nokia join hundreds of thousands of growing small and medium businesses that benefit from outsourcing their office and workplace needs to Regus, allowing them to focus on their core activities.

Over 800,000 customers a day benefit from Regus facilities spread across a global footprint of 1,100 locations in 500 cities and 87 countries, which allow individuals and companies to work wherever, however and whenever they want to.

Other Business Services

Occam Consulting Limited
Contact: Tony Childs, Director
1203, Building1, Xujiahui Lu, Shanghai
Phone: +86 1381 633 8844
Email: tony@occam.cn
Web: http://www.occam.cn

Occam has deployed over 300 China Business Training courses and counts amongst its clients' over 50 multinational companies & two governments (UK & NZ). Occam products & services are all developed in-house based on market needs & our clients requirements and goals. We have trained business people and government personnel from 30+ countries are based in Shanghai and provide services worldwide. 50% of training participants are Chinese nationals working in foreign companies and 50% are foreigners. Training can be deployed in English or Chinese.

Patent and Trademark Law Services

BEIJING KUNRONG LAW FIRM
Contact: Yi Sun, Partner
1521, Block A, Boya International Center,
No.1 Lizezhongyi Road,
Chaoyang District, Beijing, China
Phone: (86) 10 - 8478 2027-803/802/801, 10 - 5718 7871
Fax: (86) 10 - 8478 2027-808
Email: sun28564@163.com
Web: http://www.95lawyer.com

Beijing Kun Rong lawfirm has developed wide-ranging contacts and experience in all sectors of China practice and has dealt with projects throughout China for a diverse cross-section of clients.

Product Standards, Testing, and Certification

Beijing Hotwire Medical Tech Development Co., Ltd.
Contact: Matthew Zheng, Vice General Manager
Rm.308,Tower A,E-wing Center No.113,Zhichun Rd.
Haidian District 100086,Beijing,China

Phone: 0086-10-82622478 ;   0086-10-8262-8339/3934/5954
Fax: +0086-10-82628554
Email: Registration@hotwiremed.com
Web: http://www.hotwiremed.com

Beijing Hotwire Medical Tech Development Co., Ltd. is a company specialized in providing State Food and Drug Administration (SFDA and Ministry of Health (MOH) approvals regulatory registration Consulting service, like Registration for Medical Device, Healthy Food, Pharmaceuticals, Sterilization, IVD, Clinical Trial service, Translation Service, helping foreign manufacturers obtain regulatory approvals for their products to enter China Market.

China Certification Corporation
Contact: Joe Goerbert, Managing Consultant
70 West Madison St., Suite 1400
Chicago Illinois, 60602 United States
Phone: (773)-595-1767
Fax: (773)-654-2673
Email: j.goerbert@china-certification.com
Web: http://www.china-certification.com/en

China Certification Corporation provides you with all-inclusive services for any need regarding CCC export certification for China. With 7 years of experience, offices in the US, Germany and China and good contacts with authorities and test labs, clients can expect Grade-A consulting services delivered. We have conducted certification in as little as 2 months and have a 100% success track record. Call or mail us for fast and easy CCC certification.

REACH24H CONSULTING GROUP
Contact: NATHAN CHEN, Deputy General Manager
6th Floor, Building No.2, Hopson Center, No 327 Tianmushan Rd
Hangzhou Zhejiang, 310023 China
Phone: 86 13185024868
Fax: 86 13185024868
Email: nathan.chen@reach24h.ccom
Web: https://www.reach24h.com

REACH24H Group provides product Stewardship & regulatory compliance service for global customers from its three offices – Ireland, Canada and China, assisting global companies to comply with global chemical regulations including the EU REACH, China new chemical substance notification, Global GHS, USA TSCA, etc.

Shanghai Labor Environment Test Technical Consultation Co., Ltd.
Contact: Ting Zhu, Director of Business Development
No.865 Hezheng Rd. Jiading District
Shanghai, 201822 China
Phone: +(86 21) 5998 9191
Fax: +(86 21) 5998 9393
Email: zhuting0717@126.com
Web: http://www.shlabor.com/

Shanghai Labor Co. is a leading analytical laboratory for environmental testing services in China. It focuses on providing outstanding testing service, technical expertise, consultation and solution for detection of workplace hazards, hygienic for radiation, drinking water, public place and indoor environment, air and waste gas, water and wastewater and noise.
Shanghai Labor is holding accreditations from American Industrial Hygiene Association (AIHA) as an accredited Industrial Hygiene laboratory (ID: 198270); China National Accreditation Service for Conformity Assessment (CNAS); and certificates from China Metrology Accreditation and Shanghai Production Safety Supervision and Administration.

Real Estate Services

Regus Business Centre

Contact: Andrew Chen, Corporate Account Director
Silver Centre, 1388 North Shaan Xi Road
Shanghai
Phone: +86 (0) 21 6149 8016
Fax: +86 (0) 21 6149 8016
Email: AndrewLu.Chen@regus.com
Web: http://www.regus.cn

Regus is the world's largest provider of workplace solutions. Regus enables people to work their way, whether it's from home, on the road or from an office. Customers such as Google, GlaxoSmithKline, and Nokia join hundreds of thousands of growing small and medium businesses that benefit from outsourcing their office and workplace needs to Regus, allowing them to focus on their core activities.

Over 800,000 customers a day benefit from Regus facilities spread across a global footprint of 1,100 locations in 500 cities and 87 countries, which allow individuals and companies to work wherever, however and whenever they want to.

Security and Personal Safety

Hill & Associates

Contact: Iain Young, Business Development Director
6A Huamin Empire Plaza, 728 Yanan Xi Road, Shanghai, China
Phone: (86) 21 - 5238 5599
Fax: (86) 21 - 5237 1693
Email: iain.young@hill-assoc.com
Web: http://www.hill-assoc.com

Hill & Associates, a G4S company, is a globally recognized leader in enterprise risk management with a long and successful track record in China and the AP Region from Japan to Pakistan. We operate in 4 primary business units: Fraud Prevention and Integrity Risk Consulting and Advisory, Corporate Intelligence, Risk Management/Protective Security and Risk Intelligence.

Trade Show and Exhibition Services

Skyline Exhibit Systems (Shanghai) Co. Ltd
Contact: Jenny Town, GM Assistant
Building A19, 6999 Chuansha Road, Pudong New Area
Shanghai, 201202 China
Phone: 86 21 5859 9900
Fax: 86 21 5859 9662
Email: jennytown@skyline.com
Web: http://www.skyline.com/

We are a subsidiary of Skyline Exhibits Inc. in Eagan, MN. As part of Skyline Global Service Center network we provide exhibiting turnkey services, including booth design, graphic production, booth installation & dismantle, asset management, and logistic support to US companies exhibiting in China. Skyline Exhibits have the unique feature of being reusable, reconfigurable, and lightweight. You can either rent or purchase from us. We dedicate to your exhibiting success!

Translation and Interpretation

Beijing Far-Reaching Translation and Consulting Co.,Ltd
Contact: Victoria Li, Manager
Rm518,Building H, the Institute of Physics,CAS No.
8,Nansanjie,Zhongguancun,Haidian Distr.,Beijing
Phone: (86-10) 6252 2579/8265 8881
Fax: (86-10) 8264 9418
Email: translation@vip.163.com
Web: http://www.translationfirm.com

BFTCC is located in Zhongguancun, Beijing. We have served multinationals, UN agencies and high profile foreigners for 10 years. We focus on translation between Chinese and English and provide the following services: Paper translation is provided worldwide, Simultaneous interpretation, Consecutive interpretation, Escort interpretation, Additional services: creation of Chinese names and temporary secretary.

Language Solutions Co., Ltd.
Contact: Rachel Yang, Project Manager
238E, 668 Rd. Shangda, Baoshan District,
Shanghai
Phone: 0086-13761123481
Email: yangrachel@hotmail.com
Web: www.langsolutions.com.cn

Language Solutions is a professional translation and interpretation team, proficient in over 10 languages - Chinese English, German, French, Spanish, Portuguese, Arabic, Russian, Japanese, Korean, etc. We have worked with multinational business people and our customer satisfaction rate is over 95% on a scale of 100%.

TranslationTop Co., Ltd.

Contact: Vivian Lee, Project Manager
1135 Wuding Rd., Suite 1606, Jing'an District
Shanghai
Phone: (86 21) 6232 9538

Fax: (86 21) 6232 9767
Email: lyh@translationtop.com
Web: http://www.translationtop.com

Founded 2006 and based in Shanghai, we provide professional language services in 60 countries including China across 6 continents. Our multi-cultural and expert Native Speakers carved out a niche across global markets by providing the most-advanced and top solutions for various industrial sectors.

Travel Facilitation

Asia Getaway Inc.
Contact: Polly Yu, Vice President
5355 Mira Sorrento Place, Suite 230 San Diego, CA 92121
Phone: 760 635 1288
Fax: 760 635 1287
Email: info@asiagetaway.com
Web: http://asiagetaway.com

Asia Getaway Inc. specializes in organizing Trade Missions, Conferences, Trade Shows and Meetings from the U. S. to China. Since 1997, we have established long-term business relationships in China which enables us to offer great value travel programs to our clients. Our network with government offices and trade associations will further enhance the success of your business programs to China. We are totally committed to providing quality service. Asia Getaway Inc. is your partner in travel.

Chin-EASE Corp
Contact: Joanna Crain, President & CEO
#1 Guanghua Lu Xili, A-105 Beijing
Phone: 86-139-1071-4351
Email: joannacrain@Chin-EASEcorp.com
Web: http://www.Chin-EASEcorp.com

Planning a personal trip to China can be stressful; planning a business trip or event in China can be a class of stress all its own. However, with the assistance of Chin-EASE it doesn't have to be that way. Whether you're an executive needing to set up meetings with Chinese government officials and private sector representatives or wanting to hold a trade conference in China, we're here to help.

Shopping Tours Shanghai
Contact: Suzy Fewtrell, Owner
Room 1404 Building 16 58 Aomen Road, Shanghai, China 200060
Phone: +86 13817405677

Fax: +86 135 8599 1779
Email: info@shoppingtoursshanghai.com
Web: http://www.shoppingtoursshanghai.com

Shopping Tours Shanghai is the answer to all your shopping needs! We have personally hand selected the places we love to shop to give you an amazing, hassle-free shopping experience in Shanghai. From our most popular Best of Everything full or half-day group tour to a private tailored shopping excursion to meet your specific shopping requirements, we can even organise a quality tailor just to come to your hotel. Our shopping tours are a great option for a partner program or our personal shopper service can deliver all those gifts you were supposed to buy to your hotel before you leave! All our guides are native English speakers from the USA, Canada, New Zealand or Australia.

U.S. Government Staff in China

Name: William Zarit, Minister Counselor
Phone: 86 10 8531 3011
Fax: 86 10 8531 3701
Email: William.Zarit@trade.gov
Post: Beijing

Name: Christopher Quinlivan, Deputy Senior Commercial Officer
Phone: 8610 85313053
Fax: 8610 85313701
Email: Christopher.Quinlivan@trade.gov
Post: Beijing

Name: Rosemary Gallant, Principal Commercial Officer
Phone: 86 10 8531 4612
Fax: 86 10 8531 3701
Email: Rosemary.Gallant@trade.gov
Post: Beijing
Industries: Drugs/Pharmaceuticals, Health Care Services, Medical Eq.

Name: Lawrence Panigot, Criminal Investigator (Export Control Attache)
Phone: 86 135 1106 6714
Email: lawrence.panigot@trade.gov
Post: Beijing

Name: Daniel Green, Senior Trade Compliance Officer
Phone: 202-482-5687
Fax: 202-482-1576
Email: daniel.green@trade.gov
Post: Beijing

Name: Andrew Billard, Commercial Officer
Phone: (86) 10-8531-3589
Fax: (86) 10-8531-4343
Email: Andrew.Billard@trade.gov
Post: Beijing
Industries: Air Conditioning/Refrigeration Eq., Architectural/Constr./Engineering SVC, Building Products,

Environmental Technologies, Pollution Control Eq., Water Resources Eq./Services

Name: Harold Brayman, Trade Compliance Officer
Phone: 86-10-8531-3420
Email: harold.brayman@trade.gov
Post: Beijing

Name: Joshua Halpern, Commercial Officer
Phone: (86-10) 8531-4325
Fax: (86-10 8531-3949
Email: Joshua.Halpern@trade.gov
Post: Beijing

Name: Eric Hsu, Commercial Officer
Phone: 86-10-8531-3422
Fax: 86-10-8531-4343
Email: Eric.Hsu@trade.gov
Post: Beijing
Industries: Accounting Services, Biotechnology, Dental Eq., Drugs/Pharmaceuticals, Financial Services, Health Care Services, Insurance Services, Investment Services, Laboratory Scientific Instruments, Medical Eq.

Name: Nancy Kremers, Commercial Officer (Intellectual Property Rights)
Phone: 86 10 8531 4812
Fax: 86 10 8531 3322
Email: Nancy.Kremers@trade.gov
Post: Beijing

Name: Mark Lewis, Commercial Officer
Phone: 8610-8531-3280
Fax: 8610-8531-3701
Email: Mark.Lewis@trade.gov
Post: Beijing
Industries: Books/Periodicals, Education/Training Services, Films/Videos, Investment Services, Regulations, Travel and Tourism Industries

Name: Linda Minsker, Senior Criminal Investigator (ECO)
Phone: 8610 8531 4484
Fax: 8610 8531 3330
Email: linda.minsker@trade.gov
Post: Beijing

Name: David Murphy, Commercial Officer
Phone: 86 10 8531-3129
Fax: 86 10 8531-4343
Email: David.Murphy@trade.gov
Post: Beijing
Industries: Agricultural Machinery & Eq., Agricultural Products, Agricultural Services, Apparel, Audio/Visual Eq., Education/Training Services, Food Processing/Packaging Eq., General Industrial Eq./Supplies, General Services, Security/Safety Eq., Trade Promotion Services, Travel and Tourism Industries

Name: Elizabeth Shieh, Commercial Officer
Phone: 8610-8531 3423
Fax: 8610-8531 3701
Email: Elizabeth.Shieh@trade.gov
Post: Beijing
Industries: Architectural/Constr./Engineering SVC, Pollution Control Eq., Water Resources Eq./Services

Name: Yue Cao, Senior Commercial Specialist
Phone: (86-10) 8531-4796
Fax: (86-10) 8531-4343
Email: Yue.Cao@trade.gov
Post: Beijing
Industries: Electrical Power Systems

Name: Aiqun Peng, Senior Commercial Specialist
Phone: 86-10-8531 3947
Fax: 86-10-8531 4343
Email: Aiqun.Peng@trade.gov
Post: Beijing
Industries: Aircraft/Aircraft Parts, Airport/Ground Support Eq., Aviation Services, Railroad Eq.

Name: Xiaolei Wan, Senior Commercial Specialist
Phone: (86-10) 8531 4534
Fax: (86-10) 8531 3701
Email: Xiaolei.Wan@trade.gov
Post: Beijing

Name: Jianhong Wang, Senior Commercial Specialist
Phone: (86-10) 8531 3424
Fax: (86-10) 8531 4343

Email: Jianhong.Wang@trade.gov
Post: Beijing
Industries: Chemical Production Machinery, Coal, Iron/Steel, Mining Industry Eq., Non-Ferrous Metals, Oil/Gas Field Machinery, Oil/Gas/Mineral Prod/Explor Serv., Pumps/Valves/Compressors

Name: Lisa Wang, Senior Import Administration Officer
Phone: 86-10-8531-3945
Fax: 86-10-8531-4333
Email: Lisa.Wang@trade.gov
Post: Beijing

Name: Shujuan Cao, Commercial Specialist
Phone: (8610) 8531 4463
Fax: (86-10) 8531 3701
Email: Shujuan.Cao@trade.gov
Post: Beijing
Industries: Architectural/Constr./Engineering SVC, Building Products, Construction Eq.

Name: Yahong Li, Budget Analyst
Phone: 8610-8531 4264
Fax: 8610-8531 4343
Email: Yahong.Li@trade.gov
Post: Beijing

Name: Yan Shen, Commercial Specialist
Phone: (86-10) 8531 3554
Fax: (86-10) 8531 3701
Email: Yan.Shen@trade.gov
Post: Beijing
Industries: Apparel, Cosmetics/Toiletries, Foods - Processed, Footwear, Franchising, General Consumer Goods, Giftware, Household Consumer Goods, Jewelry, Musical Instruments, Pet Foods/Supp., Sporting Goods/Recreational Eq., Textile Fabrics, Textile Products - Made-Up, Toys/Games

Name: Yi Wang, Commercial Specialist
Phone: (86-10) 8531 4505
Fax: (86-10) 8531 3701
Email: Yi.Wang@trade.gov
Post: Beijing
Industries: Pollution Control Eq., Water Resources Eq./Services

Name: Huiling Shi, Commercial Assistant
Phone: 86 10 8531 3419
Email: Huiling.Shi@trade.gov
Post: Beijing
Industries: Regulations

Name: Jing Wei, Commercial Assistant
Phone: (86-10) 8531 4296
Fax: (86-10) 8531 3701
Email: Jing.Wei@trade.gov
Post: Beijing
Industries: Travel and Tourism Industries

Name: Zheng Xu, Commercial Assistant
Phone: (86-10) 8531 3637
Fax: (86-10) 8531 3701
Email: Zheng.Xu@trade.gov
Post: Beijing
Industries: Agricultural Machinery & Eq., Agricultural Products, Agricultural Services, Food Processing/Packaging Eq., Foods - Processed, General Industrial Eq./Supplies, Machine Tools/Metalworking Eq., Packaging Eq., Security/Safety Eq.

Name: Ming Yang, Commercial Assistant
Phone: 8610-8531 4006
Fax: 8610-8531 3701
Email: Ming.Yang@trade.gov
Post: Beijing
Industries: Environmental Technologies

Name: Qiurong Zhang, Commercial Assistant
Phone: (86-10)8531 4263
Fax: (86-10)8531 4343
Email: Qiurong.Zhang@trade.gov
Post: Beijing
Industries: Aircraft/Aircraft Parts, Airport/Ground Support Eq., Automobile/Light Truck/Vans, Automotive Parts/Services Eq., Aviation Services, Transportation Serv. (other than Aviation), Trucks/Trailers/Buses

Name: Dekuan Liu, Driver
Phone: (86-10) 8531 3669
Email: beijing.office.box@mail.doc.gov
Post: Beijing

Name: Huijun Lu, Driver
Phone: (86-10) 8531 3996
Fax: (86-10) 8531 3701
Email: beijing.office.box@mail.doc.gov
Post: Beijing

Name: Jun Lu, Driver
Phone: (86-10) 8531 3669
Fax: (86-10) 8531 3701
Email: beijing.office.box@mail.doc.gov
Post: Beijing

Name: Jie Zhang, Commercial Clerk
Phone: 8610-85314568
Fax: 8610-85314343
Email: Jie.Zhang@trade.gov
Post: Beijing

Name: William Marshak, Principal Commercial Officer
Phone: 86-28-8598 6661
Fax: 86-28-8558 9221
Email: William.Marshak@trade.gov
Post: Chengdu

Name: Ling Chen, Senior Commercial Specialist
Phone: 86-28-8598 6567
Fax: 86-28-8558 9221
Email: Ling.Chen@trade.gov
Post: Chengdu
Industries: Automobile/Light Truck/Vans, Automotive Parts/Services Eq., Chemical Production Machinery, Coal, Health Care Services, Industrial Chemicals, Iron/Steel, Machine Tools/Metalworking Eq., Medical Eq., Mining Industry Eq., Non-Ferrous Metals, Operations/Maintenance Services, Plastics Materials/Resins, Plastics Production Machinery, Pollution Control Eq., Process Controls - Industrial, Trucks/Trailers/Buses

Name: Lin Liping, Senior Commercial Specialist
Phone: 86-28-8598 6633
Fax: 86-28-8558 9221
Email: Lin.Liping@trade.gov
Post: Chengdu
Industries: Advertising Services, Apparel, Audio/Visual Eq., Books/Periodicals, Computer Software,

Computers/Peripherals, Consumer Electronics, Education/Training Services, Electronic Commerce, Electronic Components, Electronics Industry Prod/Test Eq., Films/Videos, Footwear, General Consumer Goods, General Services, Giftware, Household Consumer Goods, Information Services, Insurance Services, Jewelry, Leasing Services, Telecommunications Eq., Telecommunications Services

Name: Cui Shiyang, Senior Commercial Specialist
Phone: 86-28-8598 6546
Fax: 86-28-8558 9221
Email: Cui.Shiyang@trade.gov
Post: Chengdu
Industries: Air Conditioning/Refrigeration Eq., Aircraft/Aircraft Parts, Airport/Ground Support Eq., Architectural/Constr./Engineering SVC, Aviation Services, Building Products, Defense Industry Eq., Electrical Power Systems, Furniture, Materials Handling Machinery, Oil/Gas Field Machinery, Pumps/Valves/Compressors, Railroad Eq., Renewable Energy Eq., Security/Safety Eq., Tools - Hand/Power, Transportation Serv. (other than Aviation)

Name: Xu Tao, Systems Administrator
Phone: 86-28-8598 6533
Fax: 86-28-8558 9221
Email: Xu.Tao@trade.gov
Post: Chengdu

Name: Jianchuan Ji, Driver
Phone: 86-28-8598 6706
Fax: 86-28-8558 9221
Email: Office.Chengdu@trade.gov
Post: Chengdu

Name: Jay Biggs, Commercial Officer
Phone: (86-20) 8667-4011 ext. 630
Fax: (86-20) 8666-6409
Email: Jay.Biggs@trade.gov
Post: Guangzhou
Industries: Machine Tools/Metalworking Eq., Medical Eq.

Name: Terri Tyminski, Commercial Officer
Phone: +86-20 8667-4011 x622
Email: Terri.Tyminski@trade.gov
Post: Guangzhou

Name: Shuquan Li, Senior Commercial Specialist
Phone: 86-20 8667-4011 ext.625
Fax: 86-20 8666-6409
Email: Shuquan.Li@trade.gov
Post: Guangzhou
Industries: Agricultural Chemicals, Agricultural Machinery & Eq., Agricultural Services, Biotechnology, Commercial Fishing Eq., Cosmetics/Toiletries, Dental Eq., Drugs/Pharmaceuticals, General Science & Technology, Health Care Services, Iron/Steel, Laboratory Scientific Instruments, Marine Fisheries Products (Seafood), Medical Eq., Regulations, Veterinary Medicine Eq./Supplies

Name: Diana Liu, Senior Commercial Specialist
Phone: 86-20 8667-4011 ext.632
Fax: 86-20 8666-6409
Email: Diana.Liu@trade.gov
Post: Guangzhou
Industries: Architectural/Constr./Engineering SVC, Sporting Goods/Recreational Eq., Transportation Serv. (other than Aviation)

Name: Cathy Wang, Senior Commercial Specialist
Phone: 86-20 8667-4011 ext.616
Fax: 86-20 8666-6409
Email: Cathy.Wang@trade.gov
Post: Guangzhou
Industries: Air Conditioning/Refrigeration Eq., Environmental Technologies, Hotel/Restaurant Eq., Water Resources Eq./Services

Name: Lena Yang, Senior Commercial Specialist
Phone: 86-20 8667-4011 ext.612
Fax: 86-20 8666-6409
Email: Lena.Yang@trade.gov
Post: Guangzhou
Industries: Aircraft/Aircraft Parts, Airport/Ground Support Eq., Automobile/Light Truck/Vans, Automotive Parts/Services Eq., Aviation Services, Coal, Computer Services, Computer Software, Computers/Peripherals, Electrical Power Systems, Electronic Commerce, Electronic Components, Electronics Industry Prod/Test Eq., Information Services, Mining Industry Eq., Oil/Gas Field Machinery, Oil/Gas/Mineral Prod/Explor

Serv., Pet Foods/Supp., Renewable Energy Eq., Telecommunications Eq., Telecommunications Services
Name: Barry Zhang, Senior Commercial Specialist
Phone: +86-20-8667 4011 ext 617
Fax: +86-20-8666 6409
Email: Barry.Zhang@trade.gov
Post: Guangzhou
Industries: General Industrial Eq./Supplies, Regulations, Security/Safety Eq., Travel and Tourism Industries

Name: Eileen Bai, Commercial Specialist
Phone: 86-20 8667-4011 ext.628
Fax: 86-20 8666-6409
Email: Eileen.Bai@trade.gov
Post: Guangzhou
Industries: Books/Periodicals, Computer Software, Education/Training Services, Films/Videos, Financial Services, Household Consumer Goods

Name: Sophie Xiao, Commercial Specialist
Phone: 86-20-8667-4011 ext. 619
Fax: 86-20-8666-6409
Email: Sophie.Xiao@trade.gov
Post: Guangzhou
Industries: Automotive Parts/Services Eq., Food Processing/Packaging Eq., Franchising, Packaging Eq., Plastics Materials/Resins, Plastics Production Machinery, Printing/Graphic Arts Eq.

Name: David Averne, Commercial Officer
Phone: (84-8) 3520-4680
Fax: (84-8) 3520-4681
Email: Dave.Averne@trade.gov
Post: Shanghai

Name: Keenton Chiang, Commercial Officer
Phone: 86-21-6279-8221
Fax: 86-21-6279-7639
Email: Keenton.Chiang@trade.gov
Post: Shanghai
Industries: Accounting Services, Advertising Services, Agricultural Products, Agricultural Services, Apparel, Consumer Electronics, Cosmetics/Toiletries, Education/Training Services, Films/Videos, Financial Services, Franchising, Furniture, General Consumer Goods, General Services, Household

Consumer Goods, Insurance Services, Investment Services, Jewelry, Management Consulting Services, Musical Instruments, Pet Foods/Supp., Sporting Goods/Recreational Eq., Toys/Games, Trade Promotion Services, Travel and Tourism Industries, Veterinary Medicine Eq./Supplies

Name: Ricardo Pelaez, Commercial Officer
Phone: (86 21) 6279-7055
Fax: (86 21) 6279-7639
Email: Ricardo.Pelaez@trade.gov
Post: Shanghai
Industries: Aircraft/Aircraft   Parts,
Architectural/Constr./Engineering   SVC,   Automobile/Light
Truck/Vans, Automotive Parts/Services Eq., Aviation Services,
Building Products, Construction Eq., Electrical Power Systems,
Environmental   Technologies,   Pollution   Control   Eq.,
Port/Shipbuilding Eq., Railroad Eq., Renewable Energy Eq.,
Transportation   Serv.   (other   than   Aviation),
Trucks/Trailers/Buses

Name: Paul Taylor, Director Commercial Center
Phone: +86-21-6279-7635
Fax: +86-21-6279-7639
Email: Paul.Taylor@trade.gov
Post: Shanghai

Name: Sophie Sheng, Executive Assistant
Phone: +86 21 6279 7630 * 8557
Fax: +86 21 6279 7639
Email: Sophie.Sheng@trade.gov
Post: Shanghai

Name: Lynn Jiao, Senior Commercial Specialist
Phone: 011-86-21-6279 8750
Fax: 011-86-21-6279 7639
Email: Lynn.Jiao@trade.gov
Post: Shanghai
Industries: Biotechnology,   Dental   Eq.,
Drugs/Pharmaceuticals,   Health   Care   Services,   Laboratory
Scientific Instruments, Medical Eq.

Name: Jane Shen, Senior Commercial Specialist
Phone: 86 21 6279 7630*8718
Fax: 86 21 6279 7639
Email: Jane.Shen@trade.gov

Post: Shanghai
Industries: Computer Services, Computer Software, Computers/Peripherals, Consumer Electronics, Electronic Commerce, Information Services, Security/Safety Eq., Telecommunications Eq., Telecommunications Services

Name: Yule Show, Systems Administrator
Phone: 011-86-21-6279-8720
Fax: 011-86-21-6279-7639
Email: Yule.Show@trade.gov
Post: Shanghai

Name: Wenjuan Zhan, Commercial Specialist
Phone: 86-21-62797630*8958
Fax: 86-21-62797639
Email: Wenjuan.Zhan@trade.gov
Post: Shanghai
Industries: Education/Training Services, Financial Services

Name: Lily Zhu, Budget Analyst
Phone: 021 6279 8709
Fax: 021 6279 7639
Email: Lily.Zhu@trade.gov
Post: Shanghai

Name: Jack Kong, Commercial Assistant
Phone: (+86) 21- 62797630 ext.8770
Fax: (+86) 21- 62797639
Email: Jack.Kong@trade.gov
Post: Shanghai

Name: Yaoyi Wang, Commercial Assistant
Phone: +86-(21)-6279-8749
Fax: +86-(21)-6279-7639
Email: Yaoyi.Wang@trade.gov
Post: Shanghai

Name: Yang Liu, Commercial Specialist
Phone: 86-24-2322-1198 ext. 8143
Fax: 86-24-2322-2206
Email: Yang.Liu@trade.gov
Post: Shenyang
Industries: Agricultural Chemicals, Agricultural Machinery & Eq., Agricultural Products, Agricultural Services, Apparel, Biotechnology, Coal, Cosmetics/Toiletries, Dental Eq.,

Drugs/Pharmaceuticals, Environmental Technologies, Food Processing/Packaging Eq., Foods - Processed, Franchising, Furniture, Health Care Services, Hotel/Restaurant Eq., Household Consumer Goods, Insurance Services, Iron/Steel, Medical Eq., Oil/Gas Field Machinery, Oil/Gas/Mineral Prod/Explor Serv., Pollution Control Eq., Renewable Energy Eq., Sporting Goods/Recreational Eq., Textile Fabrics, Textile Products - Made-Up, Toys/Games, Water Resources Eq./Services

Name: June Xu, Commercial Specialist
Phone: 86-24-23221198 ext 8145
Fax: 86-24-23222206
Email: June.Xu@trade.gov
Post: Shenyang
Industries: Education/Training Services, Financial Services, Management Consulting Services

Key Leaders of China

Pres.	HU Jintao
Vice Pres.	XI Jinping
Premier, State Council	WEN Jiabao
Executive Vice Premier, State Council	LI Keqiang
Vice Premier, State Council	HUI Liangyu
Vice Premier, State Council	ZHANG Dejiang
Vice Premier, State Council	WANG Qishan
State Councilor, State Council	LIU Yandong
State Councilor, State Council	LIANG Guanglie, *Gen.*
State Councilor, State Council	MA Kai
State Councilor, State Council	MENG Jianzhu
State Councilor, State Council	DAI Bingguo
Sec. Gen., State Council	MA Kai
Chmn., Central Military Commission	HU Jintao
Chmn., National Development & Reform Commission	ZHANG Ping
Min. in Charge of the State Population & Family Planning Commission	LI Bin
Min. in Charge of the State Ethnic Affairs Commission	YANG Jing
Min. of Agriculture	HAN Changfu

Min. of Civil Affairs	LI Liguo
Min. of Commerce	CHEN Deming
Min. of Culture	CAI Wu
Min. of Education	YUAN Guiren
Min. of Environmental Protection	ZHOU Shengxian
Min. of Finance	XIE Xuren
Min. of Foreign Affairs	YANG Jiechi
Min. of Health	CHEN Zhu
Min. of Housing & Urban-Rural Development	JIANG Weixin
Min. of Human Resources & Social Security	YIN Weimin
Min. of Industry & Information Technology	MIAO Wei
Min. of Justice	WU Aiying
Min. of Land & Resources	XU Shaoshi
Min. of National Defense	LIANG Guanglie, *Gen.*
Min. of Public Security	MENG Jianzhu
Min. of Railways	SHENG Guangzu
Min. of Science & Technology	WAN Gang
Min. of State Security	GENG Huichang
Min. of Supervision	MA Wen
Min. of Transportation	YANG Chuantang
Min. of Water Resources	CHEN Lei
Auditor Gen., National Audit Office	LIU Jiayi
Governor, People's Bank of China	ZHOU Xiaochuan
Ambassador to the US	ZHANG Yesui
Permanent Representative to the UN, New York	LI Baodong
Hong Kong	
(Special Admin. Region of the People's Republic of China)	
Chief Executive	Donald TSANG Yam-kuen
Chief Sec. for Admin.	Stephen LAM Sui-lung
Sec. for Civil Service	Denise YUE Chong-

	yee
Sec. for Commerce & Economic Development	Gregory SO Kam-leung
Sec. for Constitutional & Mainland Affairs	Raymond TAM Chi-yuen
Sec. for Development	Carrie LAM Cheng Yuet-ngor
Sec. for Education	Michael SUEN Ming-yueng
Sec. for Environment	Edward YAU Tang-wah
Sec. for Finance	John TSANG Chun-wah
Sec. for Financial Services & the Treasury	K. C. CHAN Ka-keung
Sec. for Food & Health	York CHOW, *Dr.*
Sec. for Home Affairs	TSANG Tak-sing
Sec. for Justice	WONG Yan Lung
Sec. for Labor & Welfare	Matthew CHEUNG Kin-chung
Sec. for Security	Ambrose LEE Siu-kwong
Sec. for Transport & Housing	Eva CHENG
Chief Executive, Hong Kong Monetary Authority	Norman CHAN Tak-lam
Chief Justice	Geoffrey MA Tao-li
Pres., Legislative Council	Jasper TSANG Yok-sing
Commissioner of Police	TSANG Wai-hung
Commissioner, Independent Commission Against Corruption	Timothy TONG Hin-ming
Director of Audit	Benjamin TANG
Macau	
(Special Admin. Region of the People's Republic of China)	
Chief Executive	Fernando CHUI Sai-on
Sec. for Admin. & Justice	Florinda Da Rosa Silva CHAN
Sec. for Economics & Finance	Francis TAM Pak-

	yuen
Sec. for Security	CHEONG Kuoc Va
Sec. for Social Affairs & Culture	CHEONG U
Sec. for Transport & Public Works	LAU Si Io
Procurator Gen.	HO Chio Meng
Pres., Court of Final Appeal	SAM Hou Fai
Pres., Legislative Council	LAU Cheok Va
Commissioner, Audit	HO Veng On
Commissioner, Independent Commission Against Corruption	FONG Man Chong

The Internationalist®

International Business, Investment, and Travel

www.internationalist.com